General Election

UK
& P

Neil Mc
Eric Ma

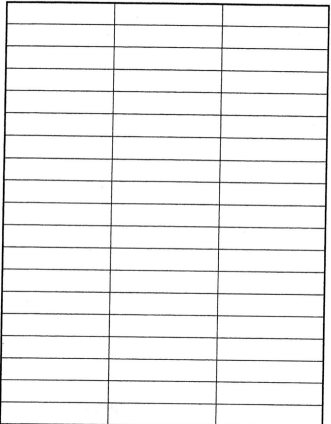

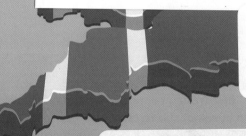

PHILIP ALLAN FOR
HODDER
EDUCATION
AN HACHETTE UK COMPANY

Philip Allan Updates, an imprint of Hodder Education, an Hachette UK company, Blenheim Court, George Street, Banbury, Oxfordshire OX16 5BH

Orders

Bookpoint Ltd, 130 Milton Park, Abingdon, Oxfordshire OX14 4SB
tel: 01235 827827
fax: 01235 400401
e-mail: education@bookpoint.co.uk

Lines are open 9.00 a.m.–5.00 p.m., Monday to Saturday, with a 24-hour message answering service. You can also order through the Hodder Education website: www.hoddereducation.co.uk

© Neil McNaughton and Eric Magee 2015

ISBN 978-1-4718-5431-6

First printed 2015
Impression number 5 4 3 2 1
Year 2019 2018 2017 2016 2015

Typeset by Integra Software Services Pvt. Ltd., Pondicherry, India

Cover photo: Onidji/Fotolia

Printed by CPI Group (UK) Ltd, Croydon, CR0 4YY

Hachette UK's policy is to use papers that are natural, renewable and recyclable products and made from wood grown in sustainable forests. The logging and manufacturing processes are expected to conform to the environmental regulations of the country of origin.

Contents

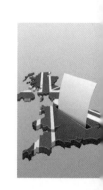

Introduction

A unique election

As 2015 dawned it was clear that the general election scheduled for 7 May was going to be possibly the most significant, certainly the most interesting, in modern times. It was to be a different kind of election for a number of reasons:

- The date of the election was known well in advance. This was the result of the passage of the Fixed Term Parliaments Act of 2011. In the past, when the election date was determined by the prime minister and was therefore uncertain, campaigns were short and it was difficult for parties to plan for them. Once it became clear that the coalition government was going to survive, everyone could put the date 7 May firmly in their diaries. The result of this was twofold. First, the campaign was longer than ever before. In practice, 1 January was the unofficial starting point, just over 4 months before election day. Second, it meant that the government was able to plan its later policies with the election in mind.

- It was to be a five-party election. The 2010 election was effectively contested by three parties, four in Scotland and Wales. Although the ultra-right British National Party (BNP), UK Independence Party (UKIP) and the Green Party, as well as several smaller ones, put up candidates for election in many places, they were never going to make a significant impact, either in terms of seats won (The Green Party won one and Respect Party another), or in terms of the votes they could win. In other words, small parties did not substantially influence the result. The 2015 election was to be different. Now five parties were to have a significant influence on the result.

- It was to be the election that broke the two-party system. On the face of it 2010 had done that, but there were important differences between 2010 and 2015. The 2010 election produced an indecisive result because the two main parties were closely matched. This had also occurred in February 1974, but it did not break the dominance of the two parties. The 2015 election, on the other hand, produced its result because of the partial fragmentation of the party system, because UKIP, the Scottish National Party (SNP) and even the Green Party were significant factors, each enjoying considerable popular support.

- This election shared one characteristic with elections in the USA. It was, to some extent, a 'pork barrel' election. British general elections were fought in the past on the basis that each of the main parties sought to secure its own core support and then to 'steal' some of the middle ground of 'floating voters', the minority who regularly switch party allegiance. These certainties had gone. Core support could no longer be relied upon — former Labour and

Conservative (as well as Liberal Democrat) supporters were moving in large numbers to support the SNP in Scotland, UKIP and the Greens in England. The response of the main parties was to offer incentives to various sections of society to support them. Americans call this 'pork barrel politics' — an allusion to the way in which sailors were fed on board ship. The favoured received a larger share of the rations from the salt pork barrel. The parties therefore offered favourable policies to such important groups as pensioners (generous high interest savings schemes and freer options on private pensions, both granted by the government), students (Labour promised to reduce tuition fees), school leavers (more apprenticeship opportunities), poorer regions (infrastructure projects such as High Speed 2 to Birmingham and Manchester to boost employment and industry), and the Scots (promises of greater autonomy).

- All three main party leaders were relatively unpopular personally. David Cameron was seen as too close to the rich and privileged, Ed Miliband lacked charisma and authority, Nick Clegg was accused of breaking promises. The more popular leaders could all be described as 'fringe politicians'. Nicola Sturgeon and Alex Salmond in Scotland, Boris Johnson, London mayor and aspirant MP, and Nigel Farage were all more popular (though opinion about Farage was very mixed).

- The debate about the desirability of the electoral system remained unresolved. On the one hand, the result produced a majority government, a quality that is always cited as the strongest characteristic of the first-past-the-post system (FPTP). On the other, it threw up two major anomalies. One was the hugely exaggerated representation of the SNP in Parliament. The other was the gross discrimination against UKIP, which won 12.6% of the vote but only one seat. Even the Liberal Democrat Party has never suffered such discrimination.

- Rarely, if ever, has an election campaign been so dominated by the opinion polls, which consistently suggested a dead heat between the two main parties and a hung parliament. This meant that much of the campaign centred around the various permutations for a coalition or minority government, as well as a good deal of negative campaigning concerning the dangers of indecisive government or excessive influence from the SNP. Rarely, too, have the polls been so wrong — this made the results both dramatic and surprising.

- The strong showing by the SNP demonstrated that the referendum of 2014 did not end the debate about Scottish independence. Indeed some have claimed that the election will come to mark the beginning of the disintegration of the United Kingdom.

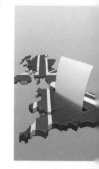

Chapter 1

The result

The overall result

The overall result of the 2015 general election is given in Table 1.1. In some ways this was a *conventional* result, i.e. typical of results before 2010. It was conventional in that:

- A majority government was elected.
- The new government won with a minority of the popular vote — about 37%.
- The gap between the governing party and the next party, Labour, was exaggerated by the electoral system.
- A party with *concentrated* support — the SNP — did well out of the FPTP system.
- Smaller parties were discriminated against — mainly UKIP, but also the Greens and the Liberal Democrats.
- The election result in Wales once again demonstrated the weakness of nationalist feeling in that country, as Plaid Cymru failed to make progress.

But it was also an *unusual* election in that:

- FPTP historically has usually produced *decisive* government majorities (1979, 1983, 1987, 1997, 2001, 2005). This election did not and has been likened to 1992 (also a surprise result), when John Major led a Conservative government with a starting majority of 21. Major encountered great difficulties as a result of his narrow majority. David Cameron's majority is even smaller, leaving him relatively more vulnerable to internal party disputes.
- One part of the country — Scotland — produced a result which was completely at odds with the rest of the UK. This immediately precipitated a constitutional crisis.
- One party — UKIP — was excessively discriminated against, possibly more so than any party in UK history. Though UKIP may well have been mortally wounded by the result, as well as by the subsequent conflict within its leadership, it has again thrown into focus the iniquities of FPTP and may reignite the electoral reform debate. Even the SNP, which benefited enormously from FPTP, retains its support for the introduction of proportional representation for general elections.

So, the outcome is a majority Conservative government, the first such government since 1992 — a government with a clear mandate and the prospect of governing alone for 5 years. But it is also a fragile government, with a slender majority, a dissident faction of right-wingers in its own ranks and several difficult pieces of legislation, negotiations to undertake and decisions to make.

Table 1.1 Overall result of the general election held on 7 May 2015

Party	Seats won	% seats	Change in seats since 2010	% votes	Change in votes since 2010
Conservative	331	51.0	+24	36.9	+0.8
Labour	232	35.7	−26	30.4	+1.5
SNP	56	8.6	+50	4.7*	+3.1
Liberal Democrat	8	1.2	−49	7.9	−15.2
Democratic Unionist (NI)	8	1.2	0	0.6*	0.0
Sinn Fein (NI)	4	0.6	−1	0.6*	0.0
Plaid Cymru	3	0.5	0	0.6*	0.0
SDLP (NI)	3	0.5	0	0.3*	0.0
Ulster Unionist (NI)	2	0.3	+2	0.4*	0.0
UKIP	1	0.2	+1	12.6	+9.5
Green Party	1	0.2	0	3.8	+2.8
Others	1	0.0	0	1.2	−2.5
Total seats	650				
Turnout	66.1%				

*These parties only put up candidates in their own countries, not in the UK as a whole so their percentage share appears lower than it was in those countries. For example, the SNP won 50% of the votes in Scotland.

The result in the national regions

England

Table 1.2 The general election result: England only

Party	Seats won	% seats won	Change in seats won since 2010	% vote	Change in % vote since 2010
Conservative	319	59.8	+21	41.0	+1.4
Labour	206	38.6	+15	31.6	+3.5
Liberal Democrat	6	1.1	−37	8.2	−16.0
UKIP	1	0.1	+1	14.1	+10.6
Green Party	1	0.1	0	4.2	+3.2
Others	0	0.0	−1**	2.7*	+0.9*
Turnout	65.9%				

* Some errors due to rounding

**This seat was lost by George Galloway and the Respect Party to Labour. However, this result is now challenged and being investigated.

From Table 1.2 we can see that the Conservative Party won more clearly in England than in the UK as a whole. This is normally the case, as Labour has, in the past, tended to dominate Wales and Scotland. What is especially noteworthy here is that, on issues that *only* affect England, if the MPs representing Scotland, Wales and Northern Ireland were to withdraw from voting in Parliament, the Conservative government would have a very comfortable majority, amounting to 105 seats. So, if the supporters of 'English Votes for English Laws' (EVEL) get their way, the government will be very comfortable on English issues.

The other interesting feature is that England after 2015 is very much a two-party system, at least as far as parliamentary seats is concerned. The smaller parties only mustered 8 out of 533 seats between them. If, on the other hand we look at votes instead of seats, we could say that England is now a five-party system.

The Conservative Party did slightly better than Labour since 2010, adding 21 seats to its tally, while Labour added only 15. However, in terms of votes, Labour did rather better than the Conservatives. Of course, the biggest loser was the Liberal Democrat Party, which lost most of its seats in England.

Scotland

Table 1.3 The general election result in Scotland

Party	Seats won	% seats won	Change in seats won since 2010	% vote	Change in % vote since 2010
SNP	56	94.9	+50	50.0	+30.0
Labour	1	1.7	−40	24.3	−17.7
Conservative	1	1.7	0	14.9	−1.8
Liberal Democrat	1	1.7	−10	7.5	−11.3
UKIP	0	0	0	1.6	+0.9
Green Party	0	0	0	1.3	+0.7
Other	0	0	0	0.4	0.0
Turnout	71.1%				

What happened in Scotland in the 2015 election was one of the most dramatic events in modern British political history (Table 1.3). Its repercussions threaten to be seismic. Never before in UK history has a political party made such rapid progress in one election, going from winning just 6 seats in 2010 to 56 in 2015. Furthermore, the SNP became the first party to win over 50% of the popular vote among its own electorate in a major election.

The outcome represented a crisis of legitimacy. Could a Conservative government lay any claim to governing Scotland when it won only one seat in the whole country, and only about 15% of the popular vote there? In addition, the result demonstrated the depth of feeling in Scotland for greater autonomy. The SNP has refused to claim it was a vote for full independence, especially as, less than 12 months before, such a change had been rejected by the electorate. In September 2014, 45% of the Scottish voters supported full independence, so, assuming all these voted for the SNP in May, the party only gathered a further 5% in the general election. Nevertheless, the vote was a clear indication that most Scots feel unhappy with the performance of London-based government, especially the coalition.

The crisis is not only constitutional. It is also political. For Labour, which lost 40 of its Scottish seats and several leading members of the party with them, it was clear that the more radical, left-of-centre policies of the SNP were more popular than Labour's (and indeed the Liberal Democrats') more moderate stance on economic and social issues. In the future, therefore, Labour has a major problem regaining its dominance in the country. If it were to adopt the more radical policies the Scots seem to demand, it would lose further support in England. In other words, it appears that Labour may have lost Scotland for a generation. As Labour relies on winning 40 or so Scottish seats to win national elections, it will find it difficult to win any general election in the foreseeable future.

Wales

Table 1.4 The general election result in Wales

Party	Seats won	% seats won	Change in seats won since 2010	% vote	Change in % vote since 2010
Labour	25	62.5	−1	36.9	+0.6
Conservative	11	27.5	+3	27.2	+1.1
Plaid Cymru	3	7.5	0	12.1	+0.9
Liberal Democrat	1	2.5	−2	6.5	−13.6
UKIP	0	0.0	0	13.6	+11.2
Green Party	0	0.0	0	2.6	+2.1
Other	0	0.0	0	1.1	0
Turnout	**65.6%**				

It was very much 'business as usual' in Wales (Table 1.4). The Conservatives gained a few seats and Labour lost one, but the political map of Wales remains largely unchanged, especially as Plaid Cymru failed to make a breakthrough on the back of the rise of nationalism in Scotland. UKIP won 13.6% of the vote but no seats, another major anomaly of the FPTP system.

Northern Ireland

Table 1.5 The general election result in Northern Ireland

Party	Seats won	% seats won	Change in seats won since 2010	% vote	Change in % vote since 2010
Democratic Unionist	8	44.4	0	25.7	+0.7
Sinn Fein	4	22.2	−1	24.5	−1.0
SDLP	3	16.7	0	13.9	−2.6
Ulster Unionist	2	11.1	+2	16.0	+0.8
Alliance	0	0.0	−1	8.6	+2.2
Others	1	5.6	0	11.3	−0.1
Turnout	58.1%				

Northern Ireland has its own, particular political system (Table 1.5). The main parties do not compete and many of the issues are regional rather than national. The main interest lay in how many seats the Democratic Unionist Party (DUP) would win. With the overall result promising to be tight, the DUP harboured hopes that it would hold the balance of power in Westminster. This would have given it a great deal of leverage over a minority Conservative administration. In the event, of course, this did not happen so the result was largely of regional interest.

The turnout was lower in Northern Ireland than anywhere else in the UK. General elections mean less there than do elections to the Northern Ireland Assembly so this was hardly surprising. The moderate Ulster Unionists gained 2 seats out of a total of 18, which was of some local significance, but once again in 2015, Northern Ireland politics remained something of a sideshow.

The result in the English regions
The general election result in the regions of England is given in Table 1.6.

Table 1.6 The general election result in the regions of England

Party	Seats won	Change since 2010	% vote	Change since 2010
London				
Conservative	27	−1	34.9	+0.4
Labour	45	+7	43.7	+7.1
Liberal Democrat	1	−6	7.7	−14.4
UKIP	0	0	8.1	+6.4
Green	0	0	4.9	+3.3
Others	0	0	0.8	−2.7

(continued)

Table 1.6 The general election result in the regions of England (continued)

Party	Seats won	Change since 2010	% vote	Change since 2010
North East England				
Conservative	3	+1	25.3	+1.6
Labour	26	+1	46.9	+3.3
Liberal Democrat	0	−2	6.5	−17.1
UKIP	0	0	16.7	+14.0
Green	0	0	3.6	+3.3
Others	0	0	0.9	−5.2
North West England				
Conservative	22	0	31.2	−0.5
Labour	51	+4	44.6	+5.2
Liberal Democrat	2	−4	6.5	−15.1
UKIP	0	0	13.6	+10.5
Green	0	0	3.2	+2.7
Others	0	0	0.7	−2.8
East Midlands				
Conservative	32	+1	43.4	+2.3
Labour	14	−1	31.6	−1.9
Liberal Democrat	0	0	5.6	−15.3
UKIP	0	0	15.8	+12.5
Green	0	0	3.0	+2.4
Other	0	0	0.6	−3.9
West Midlands				
Conservative	34	+1	41.8	+2.2
Labour	25	+1	32.9	+2.3
Liberal Democrat	0	−2	5.5	−14.9
UKIP	0	0	15.7	+11.7
Green	0	0	3.3	+2.7
Others	0	0	0.8	−4.0
Yorkshire and Humber				
Conservative	19	0	32.6	−0.2
Labour	33	+1	39.1	+4.8
Liberal Democrat	2	−1	7.1	−15.8
UKIP	0	0	16.0	+13.2
Green	0	0	3.5	+2.7
Others	0	0	1.6	−4.6

Table 1.6 The general election result in the regions of England (continued)

Party	Seats won	Change since 2010	% vote	Change since 2010
East of England				
Conservative	52	0	49.0	+1.9
Labour	4	+2	22.0	+2.4
Liberal Democrat	1	−3	8.2	−15.8
UKIP	1	+1	16.2	+12.0
Green	0	0	3.9	+2.5
Others	0	0	0.5	−2.9
South East England (not London)				
Conservative	78	+4	50.8	+ 1.5
Labour	4	0	18.3	+ 2.1
Liberal Democrat	0	−4	9.4	−16.8
UKIP	0	0	14.7	+10.6
Green	1	0	5.2	+3.7
Others	0	0	1.5	−1.1
South West England				
Conservative	51	+15	46.5	+3.7
Labour	4	0	17.7	+2.3
Liberal Democrat	0	−15	5.1	−19.6
UKIP	0	0	13.6	+9.1
Green	0	0	5.9	+4.8
Others	0	0	1.2	−0.3

London

The results in London are especially interesting. Had they been replicated throughout England, Labour would have won the election comfortably. We have to ask, therefore, why is London different?

The first conclusion is that UKIP was only a minor factor in London. Furthermore, insofar as it takes votes from other parties it tends adversely to affect the Conservatives more than Labour. However, it also appears that the drift away from the Liberal Democrats also favoured Labour more in London than it did in the rest of England.

Labour traditionally does well in London, but on this occasion the capital completely bucked the national trend. More research is needed to explain this, but it is certainly true that the Labour Party needs to study why it did so well in London to provide answers to the many questions it faces.

The North

The North of England remains solidly Labour. UKIP made considerable inroads in terms of votes but won no seats, the Conservatives made little or no progress either in votes or seats. If we consider the three northern regions together, i.e.

the North East, North West, and Yorkshire and Humber, we find the following outcome in terms of seats won by the parties:

- Labour   110
- Conservatives   44
- Liberal Democrats   2
- Others   0

The Conservatives gained just one seat in the whole northern region and won almost the same proportion of votes as in 2010. However, it should be noted that the Labour Party had hoped to win back a number of seats in the North West area and yet failed to do so, possibly because much of its potential gain in popularity was wiped out by the votes cast for UKIP. In other words, it seems that UKIP support hurt Labour in the North more than it did the Conservatives.

We will examine below the nature of the North–South divide in party support that exists in England and which was further emphasised in this election.

The Midlands

In the two Midlands regions — East and West — considered here, the picture is more evenly divided between the two main parties than in the North or the South. The figures show this in terms of seats won:

- Conservative   66
- Labour   39
- Others   0

Once again, however, Labour's failure to win back seats in constituencies where it has traditionally done well contributed greatly to its overall defeat.

The East

The East of England has always been staunchly Conservative and 2015 was no exception. Labour actually gained a couple of seats but still made little impact. The most interesting feature here was the strong showing by UKIP (there are many migrant workers from Europe in the region). UKIP won 16.2% of the popular vote, but just one seat — its only seat in the whole election, retained by Douglas Carswell, who defected from the Conservative Party in 2014 and then won a by-election in Clacton.

The South East (not London)

The figures for the South East excluding London are perhaps the starkest of all with 78 out of the 83 seats held by the Conservatives. The Conservatives gained all four of the former Liberal Democrat seats in the region. It is also the home to the UK's only Green MP, Caroline Lucas, who held her seat in Brighton with an increased majority.

The South West

Like the South East, this region is solidly Conservative. It used also to be a Liberal Democrat stronghold, but the party lost all 15 of its former seats to the Conservatives. Labour held on to its four seats but made no progress.

If we now put together the three southern regions, the South East outside London, the South West and the East we see party totals as follows:

- Conservative   181
- Labour   12
- Liberal Democrat 1
- Green Party   1

The North–South divide

There has always been a stark North–South divide in English politics, but it appears to be even more pronounced with the almost complete collapse of Liberal Democrat support in the South West. When we compare the South with the Labour-dominated North we can see reflected in the statistics the wide economic, social and cultural differences that exist between them. It seems now to be impossible for any party to be able construct a programme that can appeal to significant numbers of voters in both parts of England.

The Conservatives did not win, nor Labour lose, the election in the South, nor did the North determine the outcome. One conclusion we can reach, however, is that the South West was pivotal, with all the Liberal Democrat seats going to the Conservatives. Without this change there could be no majority government.

The result in demographics

The Times newspaper, using data collected by the polling organisation, YouGov, produced statistics on the demographics of voting in the election. This research was based on polls before and during the election and may have to be updated later in the year by in-depth research. Nevertheless, the results reveal interesting features that give us clues to voting behaviour and to the differing fortunes of the parties. The statistics do not include votes for the SNP.

Voting by gender

Table 1.7 Voting according to the gender of voters

Party	% of all men	% of all women
Conservative	39	37
Labour	31	32
UKIP	15	11
Liberal Democrat	8	8
Green	4	4

Source: *The Times*, 9 May 2015

The main conclusion we can reach from the statistics given in Table 1.7 is that gender played very little role in voting behaviour, with the only significant difference occurring with UKIP voting. In 2010 slightly more women voted Labour than Conservative, and this was reversed in 2015, but the differences remain small.

Voting by age

The Times research estimated voting broken down by both age and gender. The results are shown in Table 1.8.

Table 1.8 Proportion of votes cast by age and gender

Party	Men (%)				
	18–29	30–39	40–49	50–59	60+
Conservative	34	38	38	34	46
Labour	36	31	30	35	29
UKIP	9	10	15	18	18
Lib Dem	9	9	7	7	7
Green	7	7	5	4	3
Party	Women (%)				
	18–29	30–39	40–49	50–59	60+
Conservative	32	32	34	35	44
Labour	31	36	36	34	29
UKIP	7	6	10	13	14
Lib Dem	8	8	6	8	9
Green	8	6	4	4	3

Source: *The Times*, 9 May 2015

These statistics are extremely revealing. A number of conclusions can be drawn:

- The Conservatives won the election largely because they attracted far more votes than the other parties from the over sixties. When we add the fact that the turnout among this older group is much higher than the others we have a clear explanation.
- They also reveal that there is a group — men aged 30–49 — who significantly favour the Conservatives. This may well suggest that the Conservatives do, as they themselves believe, appeal more to aspirational males. Senior Labour Party members are agreeing with this in urging the party to move back towards centre ground policies that will appeal to this group.
- UKIP also appeals more to older generations, both men and women. The natural conclusion is to suggest that older people are less tolerant of immigration than the young.
- The Greens, as was already well known, appeal more to the young, but this group show much lower turnouts, so the Green Party has a double disadvantage.

This kind of research strengthens the arguments among some parties, notably the Liberal Democrats and Greens but also some Labour supporters, that the voting age should be reduced to 16, on the assumption that this age group will reject right-wing politics.

Voting by income

No data are available at this stage on how the voting broke down in terms of income levels. However, an initial study carried out by former Labour minister, Liam Byrne, suggests that Labour lost a significant proportion of its so-called 'blue collar' vote, i.e. members of the traditional working class turned against the party and instead largely supported UKIP. Byrne's study also suggested that people of pensionable age, all over 60, swung away from Labour. Among wealthier pensioners this is to be expected, given the many incentives the previous government offered to them (a guaranteed annual increase in incomes and the ability to cash in private income funds without serious tax implications, for example). However, it appears that poorer pensioners also abandoned Labour in large numbers.

Nevertheless, Labour did perform well in London, the most affluent part of the country so it is not inevitable that income levels determine voting patterns.

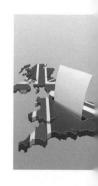

Chapter 2

Who won, who lost, and why?

The winners

The Conservative Party

This was an impressive if unexpected victory for the Conservatives. The party could not have expected to gain an overall majority. It was the first time the party had gained an overall majority in the Commons since 1992. However, it must be pointed out that the party only increased its share of the national vote by 0.8%. Yet it managed to convert this modest advance into an additional 24 seats — enough to gain it an overall majority.

The factors in its victory include:

- David Cameron seems to have won the 'leadership contest', consistently polling higher in surveys than Ed Miliband in terms of who would make the better prime minister.
- It was able to demonstrate that it could be trusted with the stewardship of the economy, having reduced the budget deficit by half in the 5 years since 2010.
- It gained widespread appeal with its commitment to help lower-paid working families in various ways and to reduce the tax burden on the middle classes.
- The promise to hold a referendum on UK membership of the EU clearly chimed with many potential UKIP supporters. So it did not lose any seats to UKIP as had once been expected.
- Many will say that it was not a case of the Conservatives winning, but more of Labour losing.
- The Conservatives took advantage, much more than Labour (outside London at least) of the collapse of the Liberal Democrats. Notably, the party won all 15 former Liberal Democrat seats in the South West. It appears that the electorate gave the Conservatives much of the credit for the successes of the coalition, while the Liberal Democrats took the blame for many of its failures.

All is not, however, set fair for the Conservatives. There remains a faction of perhaps 50 or 60 MPs who are eurosceptics and hold generally right-wing views. With a majority of only 12 the leadership may find itself in difficulties if this faction tries to force the issue in some policy areas where it is at odds with party policy. There is also a potentially divisive referendum campaign on Europe to come in 2016 or 2017. There are some senior cabinet members who may well feel unable to support UK membership. Had the party won a more comfortable majority in Parliament, this kind of factionalism would not have presented such a problem.

UK Government & Politics

The Scottish National Party (SNP)

The SNP was the biggest winner. Few would argue with that conclusion. It was the most dramatic advance by any party in the UK since the rise of the Labour Party in the early twentieth century. The party won 50% of the popular vote in Scotland and 94% of the available seats in Parliament. Yet in one sense it was a hollow victory.

Had the Conservatives *not* won an overall majority, the SNP would have held the balance of power in Westminster. This would have given it great leverage, especially when negotiating further devolution and the size of the financial grant given to the country. But it was not to be and so its influence, though important, will not often be decisive. (The Democratic Unionist Party in Northern Ireland had hoped for a similar situation had the Conservatives been able to form a minority government.)

Even so, this was an astonishing performance. The causes include:

- The Scottish referendum campaign saw 45% of the voters opting for separation. It is to be expected that most of these voters would continue to support the SNP. Many former Labour supporters stuck with the SNP because Labour opposed independence so robustly.
- There has been growing concern that the interests of Scotland are poorly represented at Westminster by any of the mainstream parties. Scotland suffered disproportionately during the recession of 2008–13 and the blame was placed at the door of all three English parties.
- The leadership of Nicola Sturgeon was undoubtedly a key factor. She campaigned powerfully and captured the imagination of the Scots. Even English voters saw her as the most impressive of the party leaders when they were surveyed.
- The Scots are mostly in favour of the UK remaining in the EU. The SNP therefore gained some votes from the Conservative Party on this particular issue.
- The SNP seems to have gained support from the Liberal Democrats for the same reasons as so many English voters abandoned them.
- Above all, the SNP success was the result of widespread Labour defections. Labour is now seen by many Scots as an 'English party', breaking the traditionally strong relationship there had been between the country and the party. Scots are proud of their traditions of industrial success, educational excellence and a strong welfare state. The country is now less convinced than in the past that Labour can support these qualities effectively.

The losers

The Labour Party

Whenever Labour loses an election, notably in 1979, 1983, 1992 and 2010, the party tends to divide between those who believe its policies were too left wing and others who say they were not left wing enough. This is already happening in 2015. The more powerful of the two arguments is that it abandoned the centre ground and this was its main fault. However, the reason for the party's poor performance (only raising its popular vote by 1.5%) is more complex. The following key problems have been identified:

- Though most agree that he improved his leadership performance during the campaign, Ed Miliband was seen as a key issue. He had developed a reputation, fuelled by much of the press, of being 'geeky', ineffectual, too left wing and being in the pocket of trade unions. His election to the party leadership in 2010 certainly had been the result of strong union support.
- Labour was seen to have presided over a period of economic crisis, between 2008 and 2010, during which the government's budget deficit rose alarmingly. The Conservative Party effectively exploited this reputation for economic irresponsibility during the campaign.
- The party failed to recapture many seats it traditionally held in the Midlands and the North West. It seems likely that many potential Labour voters switched to UKIP in these areas. The party failed to deal with the concerns of British white working-class people that their jobs and wages were being adversely affected by immigration.
- In Scotland the Labour Party was destroyed, losing 40 out of its 41 seats, all to the SNP. Apart from the fact that the party campaigned against Scottish independence and has been unenthusiastic about increased devolution, many Scots felt that Labour had, in the past, ignored the special needs of Scotland, especially as the party had presided over the decline of several important industries in the country such as steel production, engineering and shipbuilding.

There were some bright spots for Labour. The party gained 7 seats in London and increased its support in the North East. Nevertheless, it is difficult to see how it can regain support in Scotland and how it can gain a reputation for economic competence which may win back seats in England.

The Liberal Democrat Party

The election was a disaster for the party. Not only did it lose all but 8 of its parliamentary seats, it also saw most of its leadership defeated. David Laws, Ed Davey, Simon Hughes, Lynne Featherstone and Vince Cable were all rejected by the electorate. Nick Clegg himself only just retained his Sheffield seat. The Liberal Democrats also lost all their 15 seats in South West England, a former stronghold of theirs.

It is generally accepted that the electorate was unhappy about the party's role in the coalition and especially the behaviour of its leader, Nick Clegg. The party never really recovered from the shock of its breaking a firm 2010 election commitment to resist any rise in university tuition fees. Voters do not like politicians they cannot trust and they did not trust the Liberal Democrats. The party and its leader also developed a dangerous reputation for weakness by failing to mollify the Conservatives' austerity programme.

Nick Clegg resigned immediately and has been succeeded by Tim Farron. It is difficult to see how the Liberal Democrats can recover even in time for the next election.

Winners or losers?

The UK Independence Party (UKIP)

UKIP both won and lost in the election. It won in the sense that it made a major breakthrough in terms of popular support by winning 12.6% of the popular vote. However, it also lost because it managed to win only one seat in Clacton, where Douglas Carswell retained the seat he won in a by-election in 2014 after defecting from the Conservative Party.

The relative success of UKIP was a product of a number of factors. Among them were:

- The party tapped into widespread concern over the economic and social effects of increasing immigration. This was particularly felt in areas where there were large numbers of immigrants (such as Kent, Essex, East Anglia and many industrial towns in the north).
- There has been a long-term opposition in the UK to Britain's membership of the EU. It does not figure high on most people's lists of concerns, but, when combined with the immigration issue, UKIP's unambiguous opposition to UK membership had great appeal.
- The vote for UKIP was also an expression of disillusionment with Westminster politics in general. The party represented something that was untainted by popular charges of dishonesty and insincerity among traditional politicians.
- UKIP is a classic populist party. It appeals to individuals who feel that their concerns are being adversely affected by large-scale vested interests, including big business, government (especially the tax authorities), trade unions, the EU, the NHS and the welfare state in general. UKIP developed policies designed to reduce the overbearing control of such organisations. In this sense it bears some resemblance to the US Tea Party, a right-wing branch of the Republican Party.
- Nigel Farage, the party leader, proved to be a popular politician, mainly on account of his practice of plain speaking and his appeal to British patriotism.

But it still must be stressed that UKIP failed to make its hoped-for breakthrough in the House of Commons. It had envisaged holding the balance of power in Westminster, but the majority Conservative government has put an end to that. Should the UK vote to remain inside the EU it is difficult to see UKIP's appeal being retained in the future.

Chapter 3

How did FPTP affect the result and should there be electoral reform?

The case for change after 2015

There have long been concerns about the impact of the first-past-the-post (FPTP) system in British general elections. Among them have been these:

- The system delivers a disproportionate vote with some parties having their support exaggerated in terms of seats won, and other parties being discriminated against.
- Many votes are wasted. In safe seats, where one party is bound to win the majority of seats, the voters feel powerless. Those who support parties that cannot possibly win a constituency find their votes are worthless.
- It makes votes have unequal value. Voters in marginal seats feel empowered and their votes are worth more than those in safe seats who are impotent to affect the outcome.
- Governments are always elected without winning more than 50% of the voters' support. In other words, it is always true in the UK that more people voted *against* the governing party than for it. The only exception was 2010, when the two coalition parties between them had gained over half the popular votes, but its legitimacy was in question as *nobody* had actually voted for the coalition specifically or for its political programme.
- In many constituencies voters, faced with the prospect of their vote being wasted, may abandon their first choice party in favour of another in order to have a say in the result. This happened to many former Liberal Democrat voters in the election. This is known as tactical voting.
- In more than half the constituencies the winning MP received less than half the votes, so their authority to represent their constituency is questionable.

The 2015 election re-confirmed these concerns (Box 3.1) and threw up two especially startling features:

- Despite gaining 12.6% of the popular vote UKIP won only one seat. This means that several million voters have been effectively disenfranchised.
- The Scottish National Party won 50% of the vote in Scotland, but won over 94% of the seats in that country. Thus an impressive result was turned into a massive victory which is not justified by the numbers.

Katie Ghorse, the chief executive of the Electoral Reform Society, a leading think tank and pressure group on elections, delivered a harsh criticism of first-past-the-post shortly after the election:

> This election is the nail in the coffin for our voting system. FPTP was designed for a time when nearly everyone voted for one of the two biggest parties. But people have changed and our system cannot cope…The Conservatives have won a majority in parliament on not much more than a third of the vote. So while the prospect of a hung parliament has receded, the problems with our voting system have remained in the foreground.
>
> It cannot be right that it takes 26,000 votes to elect an MP from one party and almost four million to elect an MP from another. Millions will have woken up on Friday morning to find their voices effectively haven't been heard. At a time when more and more people are turning away from politics, our broken voting system is making it worse.
>
> Another blight on our democracy is the existence of safe seats. More than half of us live in constituencies where the result was a foregone conclusion. A fairer, more proportional system would eradicate safe seats once and for all.
>
> The SNP seem dominant in Scotland, winning 56 of 59 seats. You'd be forgiven for thinking that nearly everyone voted for the SNP in Scotland. In reality, only half did.
>
> One of the features of our broken voting system is that it accentuates divides. For instance, those who vote Conservative in Scotland have gone almost unrepresented, as have Labour voters in rural southern constituencies or Conservative voters in northern urban seats. The UK is at a constitutional crossroads, so the last thing we need is a voting system that pits nations and regions against each other.

Source: *Guardian*, 9 May 2015

An interesting statistic that illustrates the disproportionality of the electoral system can be shown by dividing the number of total votes won by each party by the number of seats the parties won. This is often described as 'votes per seat.' It shows how votes are of unequal value. Table 3.1 shows this calculation: the figures speak for themselves.

Table 3.1 Votes per seat

Party	Total votes for each party divided by total seats won (i.e. how many votes were needed to win a seat for the party)
SNP	25,972
Conservative	34,244
Labour	40,290
Plaid Cymru	60,564
Green Party	1,157,613
UKIP	3,881,129

Finally, we should consider the longer-term trends in the performance of the winning party. Table 3.2 shows the proportion of the national vote won by the party that won the most seats in the House of Commons. In all cases except 2010, the largest party was also the majority party and formed the government.

Table 3.2 Performance of the largest party in general elections

Year	Largest party	% of the national vote gained
1979	Conservative	43.9
1983	Conservative	42.4
1992	Conservative	42.2
1997	Labour	43.2
2001	Labour	40.7
2005	Labour	35.2
2010	Conservative	36.1
2015	Conservative	36.9

Here we can see a remarkable change occurring at the start of the current century. The leading party has won a considerably smaller share of the national vote in the last three elections. This is partly the result of the fragmentation of the electorate as well, perhaps, as a sign of disillusionment with two-party politics and the performance of the two large parties. It is also a trend that challenges the democratic legitimacy of recent governments.

The case against change after 2015

While the case for electoral reform is complex and has many features, the case against change, to retain FPTP is both simple and powerful. Arguably, too, the case was strengthened by the experience of 2010–15. The key points are these:

- Despite the 'blip' of 2010, FPTP has returned to delivering single-party government, able to be decisive and to deliver its political programme.
- Single-party government has a clear mandate and can be made more effectively accountable.
- Coalition government, though it proved to be stable and lasted its full 5-year term, was, at times, confusing and muddled, notably over such issues as tuition fees, constitutional reform, welfare and tax reform.
- With the progress made by smaller parties, the importance of a system that favours the two main parties has become more significant. Any proportional system in the current circumstances would fail to produce majority government and could result in longer periods of political stalemate and confusion (Table 3.3). In other words, the fragmentation of the party system is as much an argument *against* reform as *for* it.
- The referendum on an alternative system (the alternative vote) was decisively rejected by the electorate in 2011.

- Campaigners in favour of reform say that a proportional system would be more democratic. However, it could also be argued, that a system involving minority governments or coalitions, with no clear electoral mandate or lines of accountability would also be undemocratic.

In summary, therefore, the 2015 election has certainly 'spiced up' the debate on electoral reform, but the path ahead does not seem any clearer.

What would have happened under PR?

A further interesting aspect of the election was provided by the Electoral Reform Society in its report of 1 June on the election (Table 3.3). The society commissioned the polling organisation YouGov to ask a sample of 40,000 voters how they would have voted had a proportional system been used. The systems chosen were:
- the **d'Hondt** method, common in Europe, which asks voters to choose from lists of candidates provided by the parties rather than in individual constituencies
- the single transferable vote system, where there are multi-member constituencies, as used in Northern Ireland elections and Scottish local government

The results are shown in Table 3.3.

Table 3.3 Likely result of the 2015 general election had a strict proportional representation system been used

Party	Seats won under the d'Hondt list system	Seats won under STV	Seats won in the real election
Conservative	242	276	331
Labour	208	236	232
UKIP	80	54	1
Liberal Democrats	47	26	8
SNP	30	34	56
Green Party	20	3	1
Plaid Cymru	5	3	3
Others	18	18	18

Source: Electoral Reform Society, *The 2015 General Election: A Voting System in Crisis*, 1 June 2015 (in association with YouGov)

It is noteworthy from Table 3.3 that forming any sort of government with a hope of commanding the support of the House of Commons would be extremely difficult. Indeed, the arithmetic shows that it would not be possible for any coalition of two parties to hold a majority of the seats using the list system (a Conservative–UKIP coalition would still command only 322 seats between them, 4 short of an overall majority), while under STV a Conservative–UKIP coalition would hold a tiny majority. Any stable majority coalition would therefore have to include at least three parties. It also shows that the SNP would become considerably less significant than it is currently. The Green Party would have some reasonable representation, not far behind the SNP. The Liberal Democrats, meanwhile, would not suffer quite the same degree of meltdown under either alternative system.

Conclusions

The same Electoral Reform Society report that produced the statistics in Table 3.3 also pointed out several other anomalies:

- 50% of votes in the election — 22 million — went to losing candidates
- 2.8 million voters were likely to have voted 'tactically'
- the election saw an MP win on the lowest vote share in electoral history — 24.5% in Belfast South
- 331 of 650 MPs were elected on under 50% of the vote, and 191 with the support of less than 30% of the electorate

Despite the apparent iniquities the prospects for electoral reform remain remote. Indeed, Margaret Beckett MP, a former deputy leader of the Labour Party, said in response to the report of the Electoral Reform Society:

> One of the virtues of our present system is that the British people understand it, they know how to work it. In 2010 they didn't like any of us and they didn't give any of us a majority. But in 2015 they said 'hang on a minute, we'd rather have a majority government of one or the other, than a mess'.

When politicians from a party which has been excluded from power by the first-past-the-post system do not support change, it is unlikely to occur in the foreseeable future. However, many people have signed a petition now being organised by the smaller parties to call for reform.

It was only in 2011 that a referendum resoundingly rejected reform and, perhaps more significantly, the fact that first-past-the-post delivered a majority, single-party government, after its failure to do so in 2010, may well dull the appetite for the introduction of proportional representation which would guarantee a hung parliament and possibly too much uncertainty about government formation. Many commentators, indeed, believe that one of the reasons there was a late surge in favour of the Conservatives was because many voters had no desire to see another coalition or a minority government, preferring a majority administration. In this sense the people seem unlikely to vote for a change in the future and the Conservative government will certainly have little desire to change a system that gives it such an advantage. The same applies to Labour.

One interesting footnote is the SNP, which needed the lowest number of votes on average to win a seat, nevertheless supports a change to proportional representation. This demonstrates that not all politicians only support policies that favour themselves.

Constitutional implications of the result in Scotland

Devolution

The most striking aspect of the election was the SNP's advance in Scotland. After the close result of the referendum on Scottish independence in 2014 and as a result of promises made in the campaign before it, there was always going to be the need for a new relationship between Scotland and the rest of the UK.

The incoming Conservative government was committed to the recommendations of the Smith Commission on devolution which reported on 27 November 2014. Wide powers had already been devolved to Scotland in 1997. These included:

- health
- education
- policing, courts and law making
- transport

The Smith Commission proposed to extend devolution and change the relationship between Scotland and the UK, as outlined below.

Governance

- The existence of the Scottish Parliament and government should be laid down in UK law. The legislation will state that they are permanent. This does not quite *entrench* devolution — that is not possible in the UK because Parliament is sovereign and can undo in the future what it has done now. Nevertheless, such a law would be the nearest possible thing to making devolution fully entrenched.
- The Scottish Parliament will be allowed to change the franchise (possibly reducing the minimum voting age to 16), or the electoral system for Scottish parliamentary elections (not to Westminster), or the number of constituencies for the Scottish Parliament. However, any such measures will require a two-thirds majority vote in the Scottish Parliament.
- Ministers in the Scottish government will have the right to participate in forming the UK government's negotiating position with the European Union in matters where Scotland may be affected by such developments.

Devolved powers

- The Scottish Parliament and government will have powers to control a large number of welfare benefits available to the people of Scotland. These include, among others, a variety of housing benefits and payments made for disability and to carers. However, they will not have power over child benefits.
- The Scottish Parliament and government will have the powers to authorise some new social security benefits as long as they do not affect the size of the total benefits budget.

- The power to organise employment creation and support schemes will be devolved to Scotland, as will the power to vary traffic regulations and enforcement.

Finance

- Although the UK government will continue to control the overall UK budget and economic management, some taxation powers will be devolved to Scotland.
- The Scottish Parliament will have the power to set income tax rates and the levels at which each rate is paid. Revenue from income tax will remain under the control of the Scottish government. The Scottish government will also have control over half the VAT received within Scotland, though it will not have the power to vary the level of VAT.
- A few other taxes will come under the control of the Scottish Parliament, notably Air Passenger Duty, but National Insurance is not to be devolved.
- The Scottish Parliament will have borrowing powers, but will only be able to borrow for the purposes of capital investment projects or to cover temporary variations in expected tax revenues. In other words, it will not be allowed to borrow to cover a regular budget deficit.
- Apart from the tax revenues that the Scottish government will control, the rest of Scottish public expenditure will be paid from a block grant awarded by the UK government. The size of the grant will be determined by the **Barnett formula**, which allows Scotland to have a higher level of expenditure per head than applies in England. This is to take into account the relative lower standards of living occurring in Scotland.

Impact of the election result on these proposals

All the main parties were committed to implementing the recommendations of the Smith Commission, but the election result in Scotland changed the political landscape of devolution. David Cameron responded immediately by asserting that he intended to grant even more powers than Smith had proposed.

In the coming months preparations will be made for further powers to be devolved and legislation passed. Commentators suggest that this will imply that there is a *quasi federal* relationship between Scotland and the UK, i.e. no actual sovereignty would be given away by the UK Parliament, but the powers transferred would be so extensive that it would *look like* federalism. Cameron also claimed he would create a devolved system more extensive than could be found anywhere else in the world.

It remains an open question whether a new Scottish devolution settlement will also mean further devolution to Wales and Northern Ireland. The appetite for such change is undoubtedly less acute than in Scotland, but David Cameron has intimated that he would be sympathetic to a more general devolution settlement.

The English (West Lothian) question

The famous **West Lothian** or **English question** can be summarised as this:

- There are several areas of government responsibility which apply *only* to England. These include, for example, health, education and transport policy.

However, the UK Parliament contains many MPs who represent constituencies in Scotland, Wales and Northern Ireland. Such MPs have no mandate to legislate in these England-only areas of responsibility.

■ It is also true that MPs representing constituencies in Scotland, Wales and Northern Ireland have the right to legislate on English issues, while MPs representing English constituencies *do not* have the right to legislate on devolved issues in those countries.

■ This means that MPs in the same House of Commons have unequal powers.

The UK constitution has no answer to the question of what to do about this conundrum. The new government does, however, have plans to try to solve it. The main proposal is known as **English Votes for English Laws (EVEL)**. This idea suggests that, when English-only matters are being considered in the House of Commons, MPs from Scotland, Wales and Northern Ireland would withdraw. In other words, only MPs representing English constituencies would vote on such laws.

An interesting implication of EVEL is that the Conservative government enjoys an English majority of 105 in the House of Commons (Table 1.2). Therefore, the government would enjoy a much more comfortable Commons majority for such issues than for matters affecting the whole of the United Kingdom (a majority of only 12). So it is easy to see why this solution is so attractive to the Conservative leadership.

The problem with EVEL is that the SNP leadership is arguing that its MPs have the right to vote on all issues if they wish, and furthermore, that very few issues do not affect Scotland in some way, even if that effect is tenuous. For example, Nicola Sturgeon has argued that *any* matter which involves public expenditure must affect Scotland as money spent in England takes away potential spending in Scotland. So, the occasions when Scottish MPs would withdraw would be relatively rare. As yet it is not clear what position Plaid Cymru and the Northern Ireland parties will take on the issue.

This constitutional crisis, along with the final devolution settlement, is likely to dominate the early months of the new government. Fortunately for the government, it does enjoy an overall majority so the behaviour of MPs from countries outside England may not affect any outcomes. The position would have been very different had there been a hung parliament.

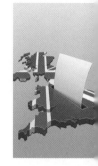

One further issue has emerged in relation to Scotland. This concerns the impending referendum on British membership of the European Union. Nicola Sturgeon has argued that if the UK, as a whole, votes to leave the EU but the Scottish people vote to stay in, there will be a constitutional crisis. She takes the view that it would be unacceptable to bring a country out of the EU if its people show that they do not wish to leave. The same would also apply to Wales and Northern Ireland. It is unthinkable that her wish will be granted by the UK Parliament but she does raise a key issue. The momentum for Scottish independence is already growing — a crisis of this kind could tip the Scots over the edge towards almost open revolt.

Chapter 5

The campaign

Negative campaigning

The introduction of a fixed-term parliament, replacing the centuries-old practice of allowing the prime minister to choose the date of the general election, meant that everyone knew when the vote would take place. It was feared that this would result in a longer than normal campaign, and so it proved. Without any formal agreement, it seemed that the party leaders decided that, once the Christmas holidays were over in early January, the gun had been sounded. So it was to be a 4-month campaign. It helped that there was little legislation going through Parliament (indeed, it became known as a 'lame duck' parliament, a term commonly used for US presidents who cannot seek re-election after 8 years in office and so lose their authority at the end of their second term). With so little to do, politicians could give their full attention to the coming election.

From the beginning it became clear that much of the campaigning was to be negative in character. Negative campaigning refers to the practice of concentrating on the faults in the other parties' policies or records in office — where that applies — rather than presenting a *positive* set of ideas and programmes. For example, the Conservatives continued to argue that Labour in office had proved to be reckless with the economy and had been instrumental in causing the 2008 financial crisis as a result of growing public debt. In retaliation, Labour pointed out that the Conservative-led government had failed to achieve its deficit-reduction targets and that the performance of the NHS was deteriorating.

There is much evidence to suggest the public are turned off by such negative campaigning, but the parties seemed hooked on it. Cynics argue that this was because they had little that was positive to say. Others suggested it was because there was little difference in the policies of the main parties so they had to differentiate themselves somehow. Negative campaigning was a way of doing this. Possibly the most effective example of negative campaigning occurred in the last 2 weeks. David Cameron produced several times a note that was left in 2010 by the outgoing Labour Treasury secretary, Liam Byrne, saying that there was 'no money left'. He used it to great effect in demonstrating Labour's apparent overspending while in government, particularly between 2007 and 2010.

Long-term social research will eventually discover the key factors in the campaign, but early indications suggest that the Conservatives' attacks on Labour's economic 'mismanagement' were more effective than Labour's suggestions that the NHS would not be safe under the Conservatives.

Looking for the centre ground

The so-called centre ground in politics refers to the majority of the population who do not support extreme ideas and who sit somewhere near the centre of the range of incomes in the country. These voters are typically middle-income families (considering themselves neither rich nor poor), who see themselves as middle class, have a reasonable standard of education, are mostly home owners and contribute most of the tax required by government without relying heavily on the welfare state, with the exception of the NHS. People in the centre ground consider themselves as neither right wing nor left wing.

In a two-party system as Britain's used to be up to 2010, it is assumed that the two main parties must compete for the support of the centre ground. Extreme policies on the right or left are guaranteed to lose them elections. This is based on a principle known as **Duverger's Law**. Maurice Duverger was a French sociologist working in the 1950s and 1960s who established a theory that where there is a plurality (first-past-the-post) electoral system and a high degree of political consensus (i.e. minimal extremist views in society) a two-party system is inevitable. The USA and Britain were his two prime examples.

Duverger's research also suggested that the two parties that dominate in such a system will inevitably compete for the same centre ground. In November 2014, former prime minister Tony Blair, in an interview with the *Wall Street Journal* suggested that it was still important to compete on this ground:

> I do think you're in a situation where there's a lot more fragmentation in the political vote, but I still believe personally there is still a majority for centre-ground politics in the UK and if you had a strong political lead that was combining the politics of aspiration with the politics of compassion, I still think that's where you could get a substantial majority...

Source: *Wall Street Journal* , 26 November 2014

Nevertheless, many commentators suggest that the UK electorate has now become extremely fragmented so that the idea of the 'centre ground' is outdated. All the UK parties were forced to confront this possibility in the campaign.

A new picture of the electorate has emerged. It looks very much like the picture shown in Table 5.1.

Table 5.1 The fragmented electorate

Social group	Typical members	Typical political concerns	Typical party support
Traditional white working class	Industrial workers Public sector workers Often skilled and semi skilled	Size and quality of public services Employment opportunities, rights and security Availability and cost of housing Pensions Personal taxation	Mostly Labour if in the public sector Considerable but less Conservative support — mostly private sector Some UKIP
White working class, low incomes	Seasonal workers Unemployed and in insecure employment Heavily welfare dependent Mostly unskilled workers	Immigration Welfare and social security Employment opportunities Availability of housing Anti-European	Labour and UKIP Some Conservative
Ethnic minorities and immigrant groups	Ethnic minority populations in large British towns and cities European migrant workers	Racial equality Employment opportunities Welfare Housing Law and order	Strongly Labour Some Conservative and Liberal Democrat
Traditional middle classes	Members of professions Small entrepreneurs Managers and supervisors Small traders Skilled industrial and craft workers Skilled independent operatives such as plumbers and electricians	Taxation Private house ownership Health and education Inflation State of the economy Law and order	Mostly Conservative if in the private sector but also considerable support for Labour from those in the public sector such as teachers and NHS workers Used to be strong for Liberal Democrats and some for Greens

Table 5.1 The fragmented electorate (continued)

Social group	Typical members	Typical political concerns	Typical party support
Nationalists	Mixed groups in Scotland and Wales, but predominantly lower middle and working class	Autonomous powers for Scotland and Wales Pro-European Welfare Inequality in public services Taxation	Largely competed for between Labour and nationalist parties
Young voters	Age groups 18–34 from all classes	Environmental issues Pro-European Employment opportunities Higher education Availability of housing	Mostly Labour and Green supporters Many abstainers

The result of this fragmentation has largely been seen in terms of a general decline in support for the main parties who were still pursuing the shrinking middle ground (not to mention general dissatisfaction with the performance of political leaders and the conduct of politics). Support for the two leading parties has declined in recent years as Table 5.2 shows:

Table 5.2 Proportion of the vote won by the two leading parties at general elections

Year	Percentage won by Labour and Conservatives
1992	77.5
1997	73.9
2001	72.4
2005	67.6
2010	65.1
2015	67.3

The decline has, however, been arrested, perhaps because both main parties are now down to their 'core' support and are failing to pick up voters from the fringes of British politics as they used to do in the past. These fringe groups now have their own parties that reflect their concerns, notably UKIP, the SNP and the Green Party, with the Liberal Democrats now rather squeezed out.

However, fragmentation also meant that the parties had to face two new problems:

- They were often forced to fight on two or more fronts at the same time. For example, Conservatives fighting against Labour and UKIP, Labour fighting against Conservatives and nationalists in Scotland and Wales.
- There were growing regional variations in party support so that elections would have to be fought more on a constituency-by-constituency basis. For example, Labour did well in London, but conspicuously poorly in 'Middle England', while the Conservatives made gains in the South West, largely at the expense of the Liberal Democrats.

The parties

The Conservative Party

The Conservative Party found itself defending its record, largely ignoring the contribution made by the Liberal Democrats in the coalition. The thrust of its campaign concentrated on the following issues:

- The government had been highly successful in its economic policies, especially reducing the size of the annual government deficit by about half. Though it missed its deficit reduction targets it argued that the previous Labour government had left behind problems which were worse than had been estimated. Despite the austerity programme, there was healthy economic growth, falling unemployment, low inflation (falling to zero by election day), low interest rates and gradually rising living standards. The party warned that, if Labour were elected, all these achievements would be placed in jeopardy.
- David Cameron firmly wanted his party to be seen as the 'party of business', seeing future prosperity as dependent on the health of business. To this end he promised to keep corporate taxes low and to maintain a friendly environment for inward investment.
- The party promised to continue its policy of reducing the welfare budget while protecting spending on health and education. This was to be done by reducing benefits where they were seen as a disincentive to work or where they had been over-generous in the past.
- Tax would be modestly reduced for lower income groups and for middle incomes. The Conservatives were determined to oppose increasing taxes on the wealthy, as they are seen as vital to creating wealth. In addition, the party promised to abolish inheritance tax on homes worth up to £1 million.
- Education was seen as a key policy. The Conservatives see the creation of free schools as a successful policy and so promised to sponsor 500 more.
- Responding to the UKIP threat and the influence of the many eurosceptics in the party, the Conservatives promised a referendum on British membership of the EU by 2017. In the meantime, David Cameron promised to renegotiate the terms of Britain's membership, in particular allowing us to control immigration more effectively.
- In response to the rise of the SNP, the Conservative Party promised to support the devolution of greater powers, especially over taxation, to Scotland.

The Labour Party

Labour faced the overriding problem of how to counteract the charge that, in the past, the party has been economically irresponsible and, in particular, was the cause of the huge growth in government debt. This was a major problem, especially as the party wanted to protect state support for education, social security and health. This led it to place greater emphasis on the need to raise more money through taxation. Nevertheless Ed Miliband accepted that Labour would not reduce the budget deficit as quickly as the Conservatives. Its main policies were:

- A commitment to be economically responsible and to reduce the budget deficit every year it was in office.
- It promised to protect spending on education, and to increase real spending on the health system every year. It also proposed to control private sector profits in the health system.
- The party committed itself to reducing tax on the low paid and to raise more tax from the wealthy. To this end it proposed a mansion tax on properties valued at above £2 million, a rise in the top rate of tax to 50% and more measures to prevent individual and corporate tax evasion and avoidance.
- To protect workers Labour proposed to outlaw zero-hours contracts, take legal measures to stop the exploitation of migrant workers, to raise the minimum wage above the level of inflation and to give incentives for companies to pay the 'living wage' — above the minimum wage.
- Labour remained committed to the European Union and so refused to support the idea of a referendum on British membership.
- While avoiding radical policies to increase house building, Miliband committed the party to private rent control, recognising how many people have been forced to rent privately.

The Liberal Democrats

The Liberal Democrats entered the campaign with three main problems. The first was how to restore public trust, when they had failed to insist on some of their key policy commitments of 2010, especially opposition to a rise in tuition fees. All they could do was apologise and insist it would not happen again. In this regard they seem to have had little success. The second was how to persuade the electorate that they were largely responsible for the economic successes of the coalition government. Here again they found the task very difficult. Third, they had to highlight the distinctions between themselves and their former coalition partners. In attempting this they adopted the following key policies:

- On tax the party promised to bring more people than ever before out of paying income tax altogether. At the other end of the wealth scale they proposed similar measures to Labour to reduce inequality.
- The party placed itself between Labour and the Conservatives on deficit reduction, promising to reduce government debt faster than Labour but slower than the Conservatives in order to protect public services from excessive cuts.

- The Liberal Democrats proposed similar policies on health and education to Labour, protecting them against reductions in state expenditure.
- The party claimed to be running ahead of Labour on such issues as house building, bringing more people to earning above the 'living wage', fewer people on zero-hours contracts, granting free nursery places for young families and cutting harmful emissions.
- Liberal Democrats have always believed in the decentralisation of power and, to that end, proposed greater devolution to both Scotland and Wales.

UKIP

UKIP naturally placed Britain's exit from the EU as central to its other policies. Should Britain leave the EU the following benefits would ensue, it argued:

- Britain would regain control of its borders and so be able to control immigration, giving more jobs to British workers and raising wages.
- It would also be free to discriminate against immigrants on such matters as housing, welfare and employment, giving more benefits to British people.
- With Britain no longer paying contributions to the EU there would be room for more tax cuts and higher expenditure on some public services and on defence.
- Outside the EU there would be less regulation on business and industry which would be beneficial.

The problem for UKIP was mainly that its policy base was narrow and too much dependent on Britain leaving the EU. This inevitably placed a limit on its support.

The SNP and Plaid Cymru

The SNP and Plaid Cymru both campaigned for greater autonomous powers for their respective countries, as one would expect. Outside of their devolution demands, both presented themselves as left-of-centre parties with radical policies to help the low paid, boost employment, increase taxes on the wealthy, protect public services and build more houses. Both parties also opposed the renewal of the Trident nuclear deterrent.

The Green Party

The Green Party began the campaign with growing popularity, but support ebbed away during the campaign especially as its leader, Natalie Bennett, found it difficult to get the party's message across.

The party proposed radical changes in the tax system, with big reductions for lower income taxpayers and huge increases for the wealthy. It proposed severe cuts in capital spending to pay for increases in welfare, notably urging the cancellation of the Trident programme, the High Speed 2 rail development, the road building programme and airport expansion. Naturally, however, the main thrust of its policies concerned the environment, with a campaign to stop fracking and nuclear energy production, replacing them with renewable energy programmes.

Chapter 6

Campaign timeline

2015

29 January

A *Guardian* survey shows the two main parties are neck and neck and predicts that either of the two would have to form a three-party alliance to form a majority government.

27 February

The Green Party leader, Natalie Bennett, makes a hash of a radio interview and is unable to articulate her party's policy on housing, one of its key issues. As a result support for the Green Party begins to fall.

The Conservative, Labour and Liberal Democrat parties all commit themselves to increasing house building over the next 5 years.

Ed Miliband announces that Labour intends to reduce maximum university tuition fees from £9,000 to £6,000 per annum.

For the first time in 2 years UKIP support in opinion polls begins to fall.

14 March

The disputes over the composition of the proposed TV leadership debates come to a head. David Cameron refuses a one-to-one debate with Miliband and insists that all parties should be represented.

27 March

Jeremy Paxman interviews Cameron and Miliband for TV. Opinion suggests neither leader came out on top in these interviews. Cameron was assured under pressure and Miliband countered personal attacks by Paxman with some aplomb.

Both Labour and the Conservatives pledge not to raise either VAT or National Insurance rates after the election.

30 March

Parliament is dissolved.

In a dissolution statement, Cameron stressed his party's economic competence and success, contrasting it with Labour's poor economic performance and overspending before 2010.

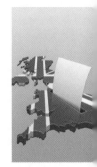

1 April

A letter, signed by 100 business leaders, appears in the *Daily Telegraph*, stating that a Labour government would be detrimental to the UK economy, sparking a debate over which party business would prefer. Miliband counters by arguing that the Conservative insistence on a referendum over UK membership of the EU was creating uncertainty and would damage business and investment. Clegg supports Miliband in this criticism.

2 April

The only televised full leadership debate of the election takes place. The leaders of the Conservative, Labour, Liberal Democrat, UK Independence, Green, Scottish National and Welsh Nationalist (Plaid Cymru) parties take part. It is carefully stage managed and there is little excitement or controversy. Afterwards polls suggest that Nicola Sturgeon of the SNP and Nigel Farage were most impressive, but the debate made relatively little impact on the campaign.

7 April

A TV debate in Scotland is generally agreed to have been another triumph for Nicola Sturgeon and went badly for Scottish Labour leader, Jim Murphy. As a result the SNP makes further progress in the opinion polls and reaches 49% support in Scotland in some polls.

8 April

Miliband announces a Labour policy to abolish so called 'non-dom status'. This is an arrangement whereby some individuals can claim tax relief by saying they are not domiciled in the UK even if they do in fact live in the country. It is seen as unfair and out-of-date, he says. At first the Conservatives criticise this idea but then change their position a day later and pledge to reduce this tax loophole, though not abolish it completely.

9 April

Defence secretary, Michael Fallon, launches a personal attack on Miliband, saying he stabbed his brother in the back (referring to his defeating his own brother David in Labour's 2010 leadership election). As a result, Fallon said, he cannot be trusted with the premiership. This is followed by widespread outrage and is seen as ill-judged. Opinion polls reveal the public is opposed to this kind of campaigning.

11 April

David Cameron announces that the Conservatives would spend an additional £8 billion per annum on the NHS. The other parties immediately say that this is uncosted and demand to know how it will be funded.

12 April

Cameron announces a proposal to abolish inheritance tax on family homes left by couples to their own children up to a value of £1 million. Clegg and Miliband criticise this, claiming that it is another example of the Conservatives reducing taxes for the wealthy.

In response, Miliband announces a Labour commitment to raise £7.5 billion per annum by draconian measures to reduce tax evasion and avoidance.

13 April

The Labour manifesto is published (see Chapter 7).

14 April

The Conservative manifesto is published (see Chapter 7).

The Green Party manifesto is published (see Chapter 7).

15 April

The Liberal Democrat manifesto is published (see Chapter 7).

The UK Independence Party manifesto is published (see Chapter 7).

16 April

A TV debate takes place including five party leaders, but with neither David Cameron nor Nick Clegg attending. It mainly features an exchange between Ed Miliband and Nicola Sturgeon, with Sturgeon urging Labour and the SNP to work together to thwart the Conservatives, but Miliband ruling out a coalition and casting doubt on the two parties' ability to work together. The renewal of Trident remained a sticking point. Snap polls said people thought Miliband and Sturgeon were most impressive. However, opinion polls later suggested the debate had had little impact.

20 April

The SNP launches its manifesto. Nicola Sturgeon, in a speech, clearly invites Labour to work with her party, partly to 'lock out' the Conservatives and partly to introduce a progressive political agenda for the whole of the UK, not just Scotland.

21 April

Former Conservative prime minister, Sir John Major, enters the campaign to warn that the SNP may hold Labour to ransom in return for its support. This, he adds, may lead to the break-up of the United Kingdom. However, this leads to a conflict among senior Conservatives as the intervention may 'talk up' the importance of the SNP and so be counter-productive.

23 April

London mayor, Boris Johnson, makes his first serious appearance in the national campaign. This is seen by some in the press as an indication of the need to reinvigorate the Conservative campaign, while others see it as a sign of Johnson's desire to succeed Cameron as Tory leader after the election.

24 April

The independent think tank, the Institute for Fiscal Studies (IFS) publishes its report on the parties' commitments on tax and public expenditure. It criticises all parties for not spelling out in enough detail how they intend to make reductions in public expenditure. This is especially true of the Conservative Party's planned cuts. However, it also states that Labour's plans will not cut the deficit substantially and that the party is vague about how it will achieve its borrowing targets. The report states that the Liberal Democrats are the most transparent and detailed about how they will achieve their deficit reduction target. The IFS says there is now a really significant difference between the Conservative proposals for deep expenditure cuts but greater success in cutting government debt, and Labour's plan which will make only modest inroads into the deficit, but will be less austere and involve far fewer cuts in public services.

On the same day, a constituency poll by Lord Ashcroft's polling organisation in Thanet South appears to show that Nigel Farage is comfortably on course to win the seat from the Conservatives.

Ed Miliband attacks David Cameron over policy in Libya, saying insufficient action was taken to stabilise the country after the fall of Gaddafi, partly aided by British military intervention. This partly gave rise to the African refugee crisis now appearing in the Mediterranean, Miliband claims. Cameron attacks Miliband for playing party politics with a humanitarian tragedy.

Nicola Sturgeon reasserts the SNP's determination to prevent the Conservatives retaining power even if they are the largest party in Parliament. Opinion polls continue to show the parties neck and neck and cannot predict which will be the largest party.

25 April

Ed Miliband reveals a Labour proposal to control private rents. Private landlords will be obliged to offer 3-year tenancies and not be allowed to raise rents above the rate of inflation during that period. There would also be curbs on property agents to prevent them exploiting both tenants and landlords. Boris Johnson criticises the policy, warning it may reduce the number of available homes for private rent.

26 April

Former Conservative pollster, Lord Ashcroft, criticises David Cameron for lacking dynamic leadership in the campaign.

27 April

Another letter appears in the *Daily Telegraph* supporting the Conservatives. This time it is signed by several thousand small-business owners. The Conservatives state their intention to spend the week talking about economic and business policy, seen as the party's main strength.

Labour announces a new policy initiative. It will cancel stamp duty (a tax levied on house purchases and based on the property's value) for at least the next 3 years, for first-time buyers on properties valued at less than £300,000.

Nicola Sturgeon reiterates her pledge that success in Scotland for the SNP will not give it a mandate to pursue full independence but rather to pursue radical, progressive policies for both Scotland and the whole of the UK.

28 April

On a day when an opinion poll by Lord Ashcroft gave the Conservatives a 6-point lead over Labour, though other polls showed the parties much closer, the Conservatives and Liberal Democrats suffered a blow when the independent Office for National Statistics (ONS) reported that economic growth had slowed down in the first quarter of 2015, down to 0.3% from previous quarters of 0.6% and 0.7%. Labour argued this showed how fragile the economic recovery is. Osborne, the chancellor, countered that this demonstrated the dangers of putting the recovery at risk if Labour were to take over.

29 April
David Cameron announces that a Conservative government would pass a law which would forbid any rises in VAT, income tax rates or National Insurance contributions until 2020. This would set in law commitments already made by the Conservatives.

An opinion poll held in Scotland suggests that the SNP is now so far ahead that the party may win all 59 seats available in the country.

30 April
The *Sun* comes out with an endorsement for the Conservative Party, but the *Scottish Sun*, its sister paper, decides to urge Scots to support the SNP.

A rift appears between the Liberal Democrats and the Conservatives with former Treasury minister, Danny Alexander (Lib Dem), claiming that the Conservatives were planning to cut child benefit and tax credits. This is denied by George Osborne.

A series of interviews with party leaders is conducted by David Dimbleby. None of the three main party leaders gains an advantage, but Cameron is forced into ruling out cuts in child benefit, albeit not convincingly. Miliband asserts that he would rather go into opposition than form a coalition or formal agreement with the SNP. Clegg says he would not go into coalition with any party that did not agree to increase education spending.

1 May
For the first time most opinion polls are now showing a slender Conservative lead, however, not big enough to give the party any realistic hope of an absolute majority in the Commons.

2 May
Nick Clegg makes a commitment that he will not enter coalition with a party that threatens to reduce public sector pay.

3 May
Several opinion polls are published and still add up to a neck and neck contest.

The issue of whether a party which comes second in terms of parliamentary seats could legitimately form a government is discussed. Commentators are divided on this issue.

David Cameron renews his pledge to hold a referendum on EU membership by 2017 while Ed Miliband says his party will stick firmly to its commitment not to do any deals with the SNP. He says his manifesto commitments will be carved into stone and the stone placed in the garden of 10 Downing Street. This device receives widespread criticism and even ridicule.

4 May

David Cameron stresses his party's commitment to raise tax thresholds. Nicola Sturgeon asserts that she would not support a new Labour government if it proposed significant cuts in public expenditure. For Plaid Cymru Leanne Wood tells the Welsh electorate that there was no guarantee that her party would support Labour, especially if it continued with austerity policies. Labour re-stresses its commitment to the NHS, suggesting the Conservatives plan more privatisation. Nick Clegg suggests that fines on banks for misconduct should be directly spent on equipment for the NHS.

Nick Clegg also claims that private conversations with Conservatives indicate that they have, in fact, given up the possibility of winning an overall majority, whatever they say publicly.

5 May

The election turns nasty in Scotland, with scuffles breaking out at meetings conducted by Labour Scottish leader, Jim Murphy, and Labour-supporting comedian, Eddie Izzard.

Another comedian, Russell Brand, having recently urged people not to vote, changes his mind and says on his YouTube network that people should vote Labour.

The Conservatives continue to argue that a vote for them is a vote for stability, but a vote for Labour is a vote for chaos.

6 May

Last campaign day. The opinion polls continue to show that the two main parties are neck and neck on 33–34% each, with a slight lift for the Liberal Democrats, up from 8% to 9–10%. The polls continue to predict an SNP landslide in Scotland.

7 May

Election day. The weather is good in most parts of the country. Normally this is said to favour Labour but this did not appear to have an impact.

The election count: notable events

- **The exit poll.** At the beginning of the evening a BBC exit poll of 11,000 respondents predicted that the Conservatives would easily be the largest party and come close to an overall majority. It also predicted an SNP landslide in Scotland and a very poor performance by the Liberal Democrats. This was in contrast to the last opinion polls, all of which predicted a very close result. In the event, the exit poll proved accurate, slightly underestimating the Conservative win.
- **The first results** indicated that the exit poll was fairly accurate.
- **Scottish results** revealed the scale of the SNP victory. Several prominent politicians in Scotland lost their seats including Danny Alexander, Liberal Democrat coalition Treasury secretary (deputy chancellor), Douglas Alexander,

shadow foreign secretary and Jim Murphy, leader of the Scottish Labour Party. Douglas Alexander was defeated in Paisley and Renfrewshire South by a 20-year-old politics student, Mhairi Black, the youngest MP at Westminster since the seventeenth century.

- **English results** revealed the scale of the Liberal Democrat defeat with several senior members of the party losing their seats, including coalition business secretary, Vince Cable, environment minister, Ed Davey, education minister, David Laws, Home Office minister, Lynne Featherstone and veteran MP, Simon Hughes.
- **UKIP** polled reasonably well at over 12% nationally, but won only one seat. The party leader, Nigel Farage failed to be elected in South Thanet.
- **A Conservative overall majority** became a certainty as dawn broke on 8 May.
- **Ed Balls**, shadow chancellor, lost his seat to complete a very disappointing night for the Labour Party.

Diary of the post-election period

8 May

At lunchtime David Cameron went to the palace to inform the queen he would be forming a majority Conservative government.

During the day Ed Miliband, Nick Clegg and Nigel Farage all announced their resignations as party leaders, though Farage later withdrew his resignation.

The press

The British press fell into its traditional positions on the whole during the campaign. On polling day the main newspapers showed the preferences given in Table 6.1.

Table 6.1 British press polling day preferences

Newspaper	Typical sales (millions)	Party supported
Sun	2.0	Conservative
Daily Mail	1.7	Conservative
Daily Mirror	0.9	Labour
Daily Telegraph	0.5	Conservative
Daily Express	0.5	UKIP
The Times	0.4	Conservative–Lib Dem coalition
Daily Star	0.4	No preference
Guardian	0.2	Labour
Independent	0.06	No preference
Scottish Sun	0.2	SNP
Scottish Daily Record	0.2	Anyone except Conservative

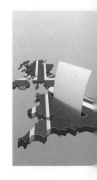

We can see that the Conservative Party enjoyed an impressive advantage in terms of press support, both from the number of papers supporting it and in respect of circulation. Though research suggests newspapers have little impact on actual voting, they do have the effect of reinforcing existing voter intentions. It may also be true that the press helped undecided and wavering voters to make up their minds, even on polling day itself. The fact that the opinion polls were so wrong, suggests some kind of very late swing and the press campaigns may well have been decisive in this regard.

Opinion polls

Opinion polls rarely figure greatly in analyses of general elections. The 2015 election was, however, different. Indeed, one of the main stories of the election was how wrong the opinion polls were. Eleven polling organisations regularly published their results and all suggested that the two main parties were very close and a hung parliament was certain. Only one polling organisation — *Survation* — claimed that its final poll, on election eve, did reveal close to the actual result. However, its findings were so far distant from other polls it chose not to publish them.

The problem with the polling 'errors' is that they may have had an impact on the election campaign and result in two respects:

- If both parties were expecting a hung parliament, it forced them to concentrate on policy positions that were affected by the need to form a coalition or to govern as a minority. Both parties claimed they were seeking an outright majority, but privately they expected a hung parliament.
- The predicted election outcome may have affected the way some people voted. With the prospect of a hung parliament and possibly indecisive government, some may have been reluctant to support smaller parties and may even have changed their allegiance to help *avoid* the possibility of a hung parliament. In practice this may have resulted in a late swing to the Conservatives to avoid a minority government or a Labour government reliant on SNP support.

Leaving aside the apparent 'polling errors' (all the polling organisations promise to hold a major inquiry into what went wrong), several issues arose from the polls. A particular feature of the election was the problem of trying to convert *national* opinion polling figures into estimated seats won by each party. This is because so many individual constituencies had special characteristics, meaning they would not follow national trends. For example, in some seats the influence of UKIP was much greater than others, usually reducing the potential Conservative vote, notably in the south, the Labour vote in the north. Similarly, the Greens could affect Labour and Liberal Democrat support. The decline in support for the Liberal Democrats was also variable in different parts of the country.

In view of this it was fortunate for election watchers that Lord Ashcroft, a former Conservative vice chairman, but now a full-time opinion pollster, engaged in regular polling in *individual* constituencies. His results highlighted these regional and local variations. He also conducted polls asking people how they were responding to the campaign. Particularly useful were Ashcroft's polls in marginal constituencies.

Elsewhere a number of national polls showed how little movement there was in support for the parties on a national level, stretching back many months before polling day. **UK Polling Report**, for example, which gathered data from all the major polling organisations, showed average figures which were identical throughout January to April 2015. These were:

- Conservative   34%
- Labour   34%
- Liberal Democrat   8%

On election eve the figures from this site were little changed:
- Conservative   34%
- Labour   33%
- Liberal Democrat   9%

Opinion polls do help people who wish to vote *tactically*. If voters wish to prevent a particular party winning a seat they may well change their vote to support an alternative candidate who can win. In 2010 tactical voting probably helped the Liberal Democrats win more seats than expected. However, in 2015, helped by opinion poll information, many voters may have turned away from the party, especially towards the Conservatives, in order to prevent a hung parliament and a Labour/SNP alliance of some kind.

On election night, when an exit poll with 11,000 respondents suggested the Conservatives would comfortably be the largest party and were close to an overall majority, it became obvious that the polls had been wrong. A major inquiry was immediately launched to find out why.

Three main explanations are likely:
- The polls were actually right, but there was a very late swing, in the last 24 hours before and on polling day, among undecided voters and that most of them chose to vote Conservative. Certainly the polling organisation, *Survation*, said that it conducted a very late poll, after all the other pollsters, which showed the result very close to what happened, but it did not publish it because it suspected it may be inaccurate, so different was it from what had gone before.
- The polling methods were wrong, perhaps not taking into account respondents who showed a party preference when questioned, but were actually still wavering or were actually undecided but forced into giving a specific answer when asked. It is unlikely that the sampling was wrong as the different organisations use different methods yet all came out with the same answers.
- Some have suggested that a significant number of people who intended to vote Conservative did not admit it to pollsters (perhaps thinking it might make them feel selfish). Therefore Conservative support was understated.

Time will tell us which of these reasons is closest to the truth.

Chapter 7

The party manifestos

The Conservative manifesto

The main thrust of the manifesto was to build on the policies adopted since 2010, i.e. bearing down further on the annual deficit and, at the same time, cutting taxes. The implication of this was that there would be severe cuts on government expenditure, probably in areas such as defence and welfare. The main proposals are outlined here.

Economy

- Running a surplus by 2018 so that the UK 'starts to pay down its debts'
- No rise in VAT, National Insurance contributions or income tax
- A crackdown on tax evasion and the 'aggressive' avoidance of tax
- Creating a 'Northern Powerhouse' through investment
- Spending £100 billion on infrastructure in the next Parliament

Jobs and employment

- Achieving full employment by helping businesses create 2 million extra jobs over the course of the next Parliament
- Creating 3 million new apprenticeships
- Giving businesses 'the most competitive taxes of any major economy'
- Replacing Jobseeker's Allowance for 18–21-year-olds with a Youth Allowance time-limited to 6 months. After that, they will have to take an apprenticeship or traineeship or do community work to claim benefits
- Requiring 40% of those entitled to take part in strike ballots to vote for a strike before industrial action can be held
- Requiring companies with more than 250 employees to publish their gender pay gap — the difference between average pay for male and female employees
- Increasing the minimum wage to £6.70 by the autumn and to £8 by the end of the decade

Taxation and welfare

- Taking everyone who earns less than £12,500 out of income tax
- Passing a new law that would mean all those working 30 hours a week and earning the minimum wage will not pay income tax on earnings
- Raising the threshold for the 40p rate of tax so that nobody under £50,000 pays the rate
- A freeze on working age benefits for 2 years from April 2016 (exemptions for disability and pensioner benefits)

- Lowering the benefit cap from £26,000 to £23,000 (with exemptions for those receiving Disability Living Allowance or the Personal Independence Payment)
- Giving working parents of 3- and 4-year-olds 30 hours of free childcare a week

Immigration

- Negotiating new EU rules so people will have to be earning in the UK for 4 years before they can claim tax credits and child benefits
- Introducing a 4-year residency requirement for social housing for EU migrants
- Ending the ability of EU jobseekers to claim any job-seeking benefits
- Requiring EU jobseekers who have not found a job within 6 months to leave
- Insist new EU member states' citizens do not have free movement rights 'until their economies have converged much more closely with existing member states'
- Cap the level of skilled migration from outside the EU at 20,700

Education and the NHS

- Spending an additional £8 billion per annum on the NHS
- Investing £7 billion over the course of the next Parliament to provide 'good school places'
- Opening at least 500 new free schools and turning failing schools into academies
- Protecting the schools budget; increasing the amount spent on schools as the number of pupils increases
- Scrapping the cap on higher education student numbers
- Integration of health and social care systems

Heritage, sport and government

- Keep major museums and galleries free to enter
- Freeze the BBC licence fee
- Guarantee those who work for a big company and the public sector entitlement to Volunteering Leave for 3 days per year
- End taxpayer-funded six-figure pay-offs for the best-paid public sector workers
- Reduce number of MPs to 600
- Introduce 'English Votes for English Laws'
- Give English MPs a veto over matters only affecting England
- Implement the recommendations of the Smith Commission, set up to consider new powers for Scotland after the independence referendum
- Increase some powers for the Welsh Assembly
- Devolve corporation tax powers to the Northern Ireland Assembly

Justice

- Toughen sentencing and reform the prison system
- Scrap the Human Rights Act, and introduce a British Bill of Rights
- Strengthen counter-terrorism powers
- Create new Extremism Disruption Orders to help target those trying to radicalise young people on social media

Pensions and inheritance

- Increasing the inheritance tax threshold for married couples and civil partners to £1 million on the family home
- Continuing to increase the state pension through the triple lock system, meaning it rises by at least 2.5%
- Capping charges on residential care
- Protecting pensioner benefits like free bus passes and the winter fuel payment

Foreign affairs and defence

- A referendum will be held by the end of 2017 on whether the UK should remain in the EU
- Protect the UK economy from further integration with the eurozone while reclaiming other powers from Europe
- Uphold commitment to spend 0.7% of gross national income on international development
- Maintain the size of the regular armed services and not reduce the army to below 82,000
- Expand armed forces reserves to 35,000
- Retain Trident and build a new a new fleet of nuclear submarines

Other policies

- Giving Parliament a free vote on repeal of the Hunting Act
- Ending any new public subsidy for onshore wind farms
- The party says it will respond to the Airports Commission's final report — but makes no specific reference to Heathrow expansion

The Labour manifesto

The Labour manifesto began with a commitment known as the 'triple lock'. This was a promise to be responsible with the nation's finances. It involved three constraints on economic policy:

- All the party's spending commitments are costed and can be paid for from the taxation and other revenues being proposed, i.e. no spending plans will involve an increase in the annual deficit
- Every year the size of the annual government deficit will be reduced
- The finances of government will come into surplus as soon as possible so that the national debt (total of accumulated debt owed by government) will begin to fall

The purpose of the triple lock was a response to attacks on the party that, in the past, it had been irresponsible with the country's finances. The main proposals are outlined here.

Taxation

- No rise in VAT
- No rise in National Insurance payments
- A new mansion tax levied on properties valued at over £2 million

- Restore a 50% rate of income tax for incomes above £150,000 (up from the previous 45%)
- A new 10% starting rate of income tax for low earners
- Retaining low taxes on business (corporation tax) by either reducing or freezing rates
- Abolish 'non-dom' status. This allowed some wealthier people to claim income tax relief by claiming they were 'non-domicile', i.e. not a permanent UK resident
- Renewed pressure on and powers for the tax authorities to combat tax evasion and avoidance
- Create a British Investment Bank to encourage funds for investment in small and medium-sized businesses

Health
- Increase health expenditure by at least £2.5 billion per annum to employ 20,000 more nurses, 8,000 more family doctors and 3,000 more midwives
- Guarantee that all patients will obtain a doctor's appointment within 48 hours
- Give as much weighting to mental health as physical health
- Speed up cancer tests to a maximum of 1 week after referral

Education
- Reduce maximum university tuition fees from £9,000 to £6,000
- Guarantee that spending on education will not be allowed to fall
- Ensure all teachers are fully qualified
- Directors of school standards to be introduced
- All school pupils to study English and maths to the age of 18

Employment
- Increase the national minimum wage to £8 per hour by 2019
- Abolish zero-hours contracts after 12 weeks of employment
- Guarantee an apprenticeship for any school leaver who has attained a satisfactory level of education
- Give tax rebates to firms that pay their workers the 'living wage' (significantly above minimum wage)

Welfare
- Free childcare for 3- and 4-year-olds to be extended from 15 to 25 hours per week
- Abolition of the 'bedroom tax' that reduces housing benefit for those who have more bedrooms than are deemed necessary in their home
- Foreign migrants will be unable to claim benefits until they have lived and worked in the UK for 2 years

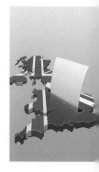

Environment
- Guarantee carbon-free creation of electricity by 2030
- Creation of an Energy Security Board to plan energy production to meet stiff targets on emissions

Foreign and defence policy

- No further powers will be transferred to the EU without a referendum on UK membership
- Replacement of Trident with a sea-based nuclear deterrent
- Guaranteeing foreign aid will not fall

The constitution

- Form a Constitutional Convention to consider constitutional reform in the UK
- Abolish the House of Lords and replace it with a 'Senate of Nations and Regions'
- Give the vote to 16- and 17-year-olds
- Devolve increasing powers, mainly financial autonomy, to Scotland, Wales, cities and regions

Other issues

- Household energy bills to be frozen until 2017
- Paid paternity leave (fathers of new babies) to be increased from 2 to 4 weeks
- Guarantee of 10,000 beat police officers for at least 3 years
- Ensure at least 200,000 new homes are built per annum

The Liberal Democrat manifesto

The main proposals are outlined here.

The economy

- To eradicate the structural deficit by 2017/18
- Set the UK on a course to reduce debt as a share of national income
- Create a fair plan to reduce the deficit by ensuring the rich pay 'their fair share' and corporations are unable to avoid 'tax responsibilities'
- Creating new fiscal rules to balance the budget, but also allow for productive investment
- Increase public spending once the budget has been balanced
- Devolve more economic decision making to local areas
- Allow high-skill immigration to support key sectors of the economy

Banking, business and energy

- Grow a competitive banking sector, supporting 'alternative finance providers'
- Prioritise small and medium-sized enterprises for any business tax cuts
- Introduce a law to set a legally binding target to bring net greenhouse gas emissions to zero by 2050
- Invest in major transport improvements and infrastructure
- Set an indicative target for 60% of electricity from renewable sources by 2030

Tax, welfare and pensions

- Raising the personal allowance to at least £12,500 by the end of the next Parliament
- Taking 'tough' action against corporate tax evasion and avoidance

- Removing a number of distortions, loopholes and excess reliefs from the tax system
- Extending free childcare to all 2 year-olds and parents near end of parental leave; providing 15 hours a week of free childcare to the parents of all 2-year-olds and aiming to increase this to 20 hours. They also want to introduce 15 hours' free childcare for all working parents with children aged between 9 months and 2 years
- Expanding shared parental leave with a 'use it or lose it' month for fathers
- Completing the introduction of the Universal Tax Credit
- Retaining the cap on household benefits
- Withdrawing eligibility for the winter fuel payment and free TV licence from pensioners who pay tax at the higher rate
- Requiring companies with more than 250 employees to publish their gender pay gap
- By 2020, requiring companies to publish the number of people paid less than the living wage
- Paying a living wage set by an independent review to workers in all central government departments and their agencies from April 2016
- Consulting on allowing employees on zero-hours contracts to request a fixed contract
- Forcing energy companies to allow people to switch suppliers in 24 hours
- Ensuring rail fares do not rise faster than inflation over the Parliament as a whole

Education
- Protect early years, school, sixth-form and college budgets
- Ensure the core curriculum is taught in every school and every child is taught by a qualified teacher
- Provide rapid support and intervention to help ensure that all schools become good or outstanding
- Increase the number of Teaching Schools
- Extend free school meals to all primary pupils
- Double the numbers of businesses hiring apprentices
- Establish an Educational Standards Authority with responsibility for curriculum content and examination standards in schools
- Increase the number of apprenticeships

NHS
- Increase NHS England's budget by £8 billion per year by 2020, with more funding for Scotland, Wales and Northern Ireland
- Invest £500 million in mental healthcare and ensure waiting time standards match those in physical healthcare
- Introduce a package of support for carers including a £250 Carer's Bonus per year
- Ensure frontline public service workers are given better training in mental health

- Repeal any parts of the Health and Social Care Act 2012 which make NHS services vulnerable to forced privatisation
- Expand evening and weekend opening for GPs and encourage phone and Skype appointments
- Introduce Minimum Unit Pricing for alcohol
- Pass a Nature Act to increase access to green space

Environment and communities
- Introduce a legally binding target for Zero Carbon Britain by 2050
- Expand accessible green space by creating new National Nature Parks
- Establish low emission zones in towns with a pollution problem
- Introduce a National Food Strategy, promoting healthy, sustainable and affordable food
- Prepare a national resilience plan to deal with a rise in global temperature
- Set 2040 target for only Ultra-Low Emission vehicles on UK roads for non-freight purposes

Housing
- Establish a goal to build 300,000 homes a year, including in ten new garden cities
- Establish new 'rent-to-own' homes where monthly payments buy a stake in the property
- Introduce 'Help to Rent' tenancy deposit loans to help young people move into their first property

Freedom and opportunity
- Create a Digital Bill of Rights
- Support a million more women who want to work by providing better childcare
- Recruit more black, Asian and minority ethnic police officers

Policing
- Scrap police and crime commissioners
- Introduce specialist drug courts and non-criminal punishments 'that help addicts get clean'
- End FGM at home and abroad in a generation
- Complete border checks and use information to improve visa rules and deport people with no right to stay

Devolution and democracy
- Introduce a £10,000 cap on donations as part of wider funding reform
- Reduce the voting age to 16
- Delivering devolution promises to Scotland
- Devolving more powers to Wales
- Pursuing a 'shared future' in Northern Ireland
- Devolving more powers in England, letting local areas take control of services they want to control

Foreign policy

- Ensure 2015 Sustainable Development Goals aim to end poverty, protect the environment and 'leave no-one behind'
- Work towards a binding global agreement on cutting emissions and stronger commitments in the EU to 50% reduction by 2030

Others

- Roll out high-speed broadband to reach 99.9% of households
- Maintain free access to national museums and galleries
- Ensure the BBC licence fee does not rise faster than inflation

The UKIP manifesto

The UKIP manifesto was inevitably dominated by the commitment to leave the EU and to bring immigration under greater control. It was a 'populist' programme, designed to appeal to groups who feel they are overly controlled by vested interests such as government, the EU, unions and large corporations. The main proposals are outlined here.

Tax and the economy

- The tax-free allowance to be increased to £13,000 per annum
- Reduce taxes on middle incomes by introducing a more graduated tax system, including 30% and 40% rates
- Abolish inheritance tax altogether
- By leaving the EU and cutting back on overseas aid the UK will be able to eliminate the deficit more quickly and reduce taxes, because the country will no longer pay contributions to the EU and developing countries

Immigration

- By leaving the EU the UK will regain control over immigration
- A 5-year embargo on immigration by unskilled workers
- An Australian-style points system that only allows people to come to live and work in the UK if they have skills the country needs and will contribute positively
- Immigrants will have to wait 5 years before having access to benefits and free care with the NHS

Welfare state issues

- Staffing in the NHS to be significantly increased
- Highly selective grammar schools to be re-introduced
- University tuition fees to be abolished for science, maths, engineering and medical courses only
- Health and social care to be fully integrated under the NHS
- Make cold calling about pensions a criminal offence
- Families will not be allowed to claim child benefit for children not resident in the UK
- The overall cap on benefits paid to families to be reduced

Governance and the political system

- Only MPs representing English constituencies will be allowed to vote on English-only issues (English Votes for English Laws)
- Introduction of proportional representation
- House of Commons select committees to have the power to veto ministerial appointments
- Parliament to be consulted before any overseas military action is undertaken
- Hold regular referendums to determine key issues following a petition with at least 2 million signatures

Other key measures

- British companies will be allowed to discriminate in favour of British workers when recruiting staff
- Abolish zero-hours contracts
- Restrictions on the sale and consumption of tobacco and alcohol to be relaxed
- Encourage the development of fracking
- Cancel the plans for new high speed trains (HS2) to Birmingham and the north
- Restrict the spread of speed cameras on roads
- Build 1 million new homes on brownfield sites
- Rejuvenate the coal industry

The Green Party manifesto

As we would expect the Green Party manifesto was dominated by environment issues. However, it also represented a very radical programme to redistribute wealth in the UK, to widen opportunities for all and to reduce government power. It was the most radical of the main parties' proposals. It should be especially noted that the Green Party does not see the need to eliminate the budget deficit and so breaks a consensus on that issue. The main proposals are outlined here.

The economy

- Increase public spending to almost half of national income
- Close taxation loopholes and crack down on tax avoidance
- Introduce a wealth tax of 1–2% on people worth £3 million or more
- Salaries above £150,000 a year to incur a 60% income tax rate
- Introduce a financial transaction tax (a 'Robin Hood' tax) on banks
- Increase the national minimum wage to a living wage for all, of £10 per hour by 2020
- Create 1 million well-paid new public sector jobs
- Reduce National Insurance contributions
- Ensure the highest wage in any business is no more than ten times the lowest

The environment and transport

- Ban fracking for shale gas
- Phase out coal-fired power and stop new nuclear reactors
- A public programme of renewables, flood defences and home insulation
- £35 billion in public investment in renewable power over the next Parliament

- Tackle emissions by scrapping the government's national roads building programme
- Subsidise public transport and return the railways to national ownership
- Stop airport expansion
- Invest in electric vehicle charging

Housing
- Abolish the 'bedroom tax'
- Provide 500,000 social rented homes by 2020
- Bring empty houses back into use
- Cap rents, introduce longer tenancies and licence landlords to provide greater protection to renters

Health
- End the 'creeping privatisation' of the NHS and repeal the government's Health and Social Care Act 2012
- Increase the overall NHS budget by £12 billion a year to overcome the current 'funding crisis'
- Increase resources for mental health to make it a greater priority

Education
- Scrap university tuition fees and invest £1.5 billion extra a year in further education
- Bring academies and free schools into the local authority system
- Introduce a free but voluntary universal early education and childcare service from birth to 7 years old
- Restore the education maintenance allowance for 16- and 17-year-olds

The Green Party would also cancel high expenditure projects such as the renewal of Trident and the HS2 plan, using the resulting savings to finance some of its tax cuts and expenditure commitments.

The SNP manifesto

Although the SNP's central policy is to secure full independence for Scotland, the manifesto concentrated on a programme which looked very much like a more left-wing version of Labour's plans, or, put another, way, it looked like a Labour manifesto of 25 years ago.

The main proposals include:
- There was no demand for full independence in the manifesto. However, the party demands greater autonomy for Scotland, notably greater powers over tax and spending
- The party strongly opposes the UK leaving the EU
- There should be an elected second chamber and the party supports the introduction of proportional representation for all elections
- Reduced National Insurance contributions for companies that pay the living wage, higher than the minimum wage

- A substantial rise in the minimum wage
- Opposition to proposed reductions in benefits for the disabled and their carers
- Opposition to proposed falls in child benefits and tax credits
- Cancellation of the 'bedroom tax'
- Opposition to the renewal of Trident nuclear submarines
- Guaranteed 50-50 representation for women on the boards of all public bodies

The Plaid Cymru manifesto

Highlights from the Plaid Cymru manifesto include:

- Full financial devolution for Wales and other powers, to be determined by the Welsh people
- Workers in large companies to be given places on boards of directors and to be charged with the task of ensuring a fairer distribution of wages
- Greater expenditure to be made available for the development of town centres in Wales
- Stronger measures against tax evasion and avoidance
- A top rate of tax of 50% for earnings above £150,000 p.a.
- Higher education to be free for all
- The railways to be brought into public ownership
- The Trident renewal plan to be scrapped
- A plan for more investment in 'green skills' to promote environmental improvements

The Northern Ireland parties' manifestos

Northern Ireland has its own specific political system. However, the prospect of a hung parliament suggested that the parties there, notably the Democratic Unionist Party (DUP), which has close links with the Conservative party, might have some influence at Westminster.

Highlights from the two main Northern Ireland parties' manifestos include:

- The DUP largely supported Conservative policies, notably on taxes and a referendum on EU membership. The party also demanded greater expenditure to be made available for tourism and agriculture in the region. One eye-catching proposal is a feasibility study for a bridge linking Northern Ireland and Scotland.
- Sinn Fein demanded an immediate injection of £1.5 billion into the economy of Northern Ireland, but the long-term demand was for greater devolution including control over most taxation and public expenditure to be transferred to the Northern Ireland government.

Consensus and conflict in 2015

A general election is a good time to take stock of where the parties stand on the key issues facing the country. By studying the manifestos and the way in which the parties conducted the campaign we can discern which policy areas enjoy a broad consensus, i.e. most or all the parties are in broad agreement, even if they disagree over details, and where there is most fundamental conflict. The adversarial attitude of parties in the election campaign can be misleading. Parties seek to demonstrate that there is a significant difference between themselves and the others, even when there is little to distinguish them.

Table 7.1 shows the main areas where there was consensus and where there was conflict between the parties in 2015.

Table 7.1 Consensus and conflict, 2015

Consensus issues	
Issue	**Detail**
Immigration control	There is a general agreement that immigration is out of control and is causing disruption in labour markets. Within that consensus, however, there are different proposals from UKIP on the right who want severe cuts in immigration and a voucher system allowing in only skilled immigrants, to the much more moderate SNP, Greens and Liberal Democrats who limit themselves to largely preventing immigrant groups from unfairly claiming benefits. All parties propose controls over the exploitation of migrant labour.
Need to bring down the government deficit	No party is suggesting the deficit should stay at its current level or grow. However, there is disagreement over the speed and scale of bringing down the deficit. The Conservatives argue it should be eliminated by 2018, while other parties have more modest targets, fearing that too much austerity will choke off the economic recovery. Only the Green Party is comfortable with the current level of debt, proposing only very modest debt reduction.
Taxes on low-income families	All parties recognise the need to bring more poor families out of paying income tax altogether. This is achieved by raising the income level at which people start paying income tax. There is slight disagreement over what level this threshold should be set at.
Protecting NHS spending	There may be differences over how the NHS should be organised, but all parties pledge to protect spending on health, keeping it *at least* at the current *real* level.
Protecting education spending	The more radical parties of the left want to see education spending rise and cuts in university tuition fees. However, the consensus view is similar to health, with no one proposing real cuts in education spending.
Housing	All parties agree on the need to increase house building, especially affordable housing. However, they disagree about how best to achieve this.
Youth employment	All parties have proposals to extend the scope of apprenticeships and other youth employment schemes.

(continued)

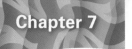

Table 7.1 Consensus and conflict, 2015 (continued)

Main areas of conflict	
Issue	**Detail**
European Union	The Conservative Party and UKIP support a referendum on British membership. As yet the Conservatives are neutral on whether to stay in (though the eurosceptic wing of the party want out), but UKIP firmly believes we should leave. The other parties are committed to keeping the UK in the EU.
Taxes on high earners	Most parties believe that taxes on very high incomes are too low and should be raised. The Conservatives and UKIP, however, argue that taxing the well off will be counter-productive and reduce wealth creation in the UK.
Welfare benefits	The Conservatives and UKIP believe that the benefits system is, in general, too generous and is a disincentive to work. They propose a variety of reductions, the main proposal being a cap of £23,000 total benefits for each family. The parties of the centre and left oppose benefit cuts, seeing them as a step towards greater inequality in Britain.
Devolution	Clearly the SNP, Plaid Cymru and Northern Ireland parties, supported by the Liberal Democrats and Green Party, want to see much greater autonomy for their countries, including most tax and spend powers devolved. The Conservatives broadly support Scottish aspirations, but resist any movement towards full independence. Labour and the Liberal Democrats also firmly support the maintenance of the union of the UK.
British Bill of Rights	Backed by UKIP, the Conservatives strongly favour the repeal of the Human Rights Act and its replacement by a British Bill of Rights. This will bring human rights back under the control of the UK Parliament and judiciary, rather than the Council of Europe and the European Court of Human Rights.
Nuclear deterrent	The Conservatives, Labour and UKIP all support the renewal of the nuclear Trident programme. This is, however, strongly opposed by the SNP, the Green Party and Plaid Cymru as well as a faction within the Labour Party. The Liberal Democrats support a limited renewal of the system.
Constitutional reform	The key issues, other than those described above, are the reform of the House of Lords and the introduction of proportional representation (PR) for general elections. There is disagreement both between and *within* parties over PR, but all parties want to see the Lords reformed. The conflict occurs over how such reform will be achieved and whether it is a priority.

Chapter 8

The social make-up of the new Parliament

There have long been criticisms of Parliament, notably the House of Commons, on the grounds that its membership is not socially representative of the whole country. This calls into question its democratic legitimacy. After the election, there were signs that this deficit was beginning to be corrected, at least in terms of ethnicity and gender.

The tables in this chapter show the social make-up of the House of Commons elected in May 2015.

Gender

Table 8.1 Gender and the new Parliament

	2015	2010
Male MPs	463	502
Female MPs	187	148

There was a small, but significant improvement in the gender balance, though much of it was accounted for by 20 new women arriving representing the SNP (Table 8.1). Women have a much higher level of representation generally in the Scottish political system. The rise in female MPs was matched by a rise in the proportion of women entering David Cameron's new cabinet.

Ethnicity

Table 8.2 Ethnicity and the new Parliament

	2015	2010
White British origin	609	623
From an ethnic minority	41	27

Source: *The Times*

Here too, a small but significant shift took place (Table 8.2). Two members of the new cabinet are from ethnic minorities. The interesting statistic here is the proportion of the *total* population from ethnic minorities. The Office for National Statistics estimated in 2011 (the last census) that 14% of the population could be classed as being from ethnic minorities. The proportion in the House of Commons in 2015 was 6.3%. So, despite the improvement there is still a considerable social deficit.

Education background

Table 8.3 School and university background and the new Parliament

Party	% private school	% state school	% Oxbridge	% other university	% no university
Conservative	48	52	34	56	9*
Labour	17	83	23	64	13
Lib Dem	14	86	13	88	0*
SNP	5	95	0	89	8*

Source: *The Times*
*Some errors due to rounding

We would expect our elected representatives to be better educated than the general population, and they are. However, we should note some significant differences between the parties in this respect (Table 8.3). It is striking that almost half the new Conservative cohort in the Commons was educated at private schools. However, 53% of Conservative MPs in 2010 were privately educated, so there has been a small drop, possibly too small to be significant. This statistic is much lower for the other parties. The Liberal Democrats have so few MPs after 2015 that the statistics are not meaningful. Labour's privately educated proportion has changed little since 2010. The differences are less pronounced when considering Oxbridge education. The Conservatives have more MPs educated there than the other parties, but there is less of a distinction. It is an interesting fact, however, that none of the 56 SNP MPs were Oxbridge educated. This is a significant figure, suggesting the SNP is a much less 'elitist' party than the others, especially as only five of them were privately educated.

Occupational background

Table 8.4 Career background of MPs in the 2015 Parliament

% business	% finance	% teaching	% manual	% politics	% other
22	15	5	3	23	32

Source: *The Times*

The most striking feature of the career backgrounds of MPs is the tiny percentage who previously had manual occupations (Table 8.4). Most of the change has occurred in the Labour Party, of course, where, in the past, the proportion has been much higher. It is also interesting to see how many come from a 'political' background, at 23%. These are people, in the main, who have worked professionally for a political party or a lobby group. It is an increasing trend.

Certainly, when assessing the degree to which the House of Commons is socially representative, it is probably the lack of MPs with a working-class background that is most striking.

Age

Contrary to common belief the average age of MPs has not changed in recent decades. Indeed, it is remarkably stable. Table 8.5 shows the average age of MPs since 1992.

Table 8.5 Average age of MPs since 1992

Year of election	Average age of MPs on taking their seat
1992	49
1997	50
2001	51
2005	51
2010	50
2015	51

A word of caution here is needed about the 2015 average age figure as some data about the new SNP members have not been collected. As it is known that many of these new MPs are younger than normal, the 2015 average age may indeed fall when all the data are available. Twenty of the new intake of 56 SNP MPs are women and their average age is much lower than that of the rest of the House. The youngest MP for centuries, certainly since the eighteenth century and maybe longer ago, was elected in 2015. This is Mhairi Black who was 20 when she won her seat in Paisley.

Chapter 9

The new government

Enhanced authority

When a party wins an overall majority in the House of Commons it has a mandate to carry out its manifesto commitments. That is the clear constitutional position. By achieving a majority of 12, the Conservatives can now govern alone. They will be accountable to Parliament and to the public without any complications arising from coalition government with another party. This kind of constitutional authority can also be described as **democratic legitimacy**.

In *political,* as opposed to *constitutional* terms, however, the authority of the government remains in some doubt for a number of reasons including the following:

- Nationalists claim it does not have authority in Scotland. The Conservatives won only one seat there and the SNP won a huge majority in terms of seats as well as a narrow overall majority in terms of votes. This is a contentious claim, only partially accepted by the new government. This is because, as far as Westminster parliamentary elections are concerned, the United Kingdom is one single political unit. If the government has the authority to govern the whole of the UK, it also has authority to govern all parts of that kingdom. The fact that David Cameron so readily and speedily began negotiations to grant Scotland wide autonomous powers is an indication of this ambiguity over authority.

- The Conservatives won just under 37% of the national vote. This cannot be described as a ringing endorsement and supporters of electoral reform insist that such a low plurality as 37% does not give authority to the government to do exactly as it wishes. Orthodox supporters of constitutional rule, however, say that this is not relevant. It is seats in the Commons that count, not national votes.

- With such a small majority the government may well find itself in difficulties when trying to pass contentious legislation. It will only take a handful of its own members to 'cross the floor' and vote with the opposition for such legislation to be blocked. Indeed this reality may well have been behind David Cameron's decision to postpone, and perhaps abandon, proposals to repeal the Human Rights Act and introduce a British Bill of Rights in its place. In other words, the authority of the government exists, but it is a fragile authority.

Set against these doubts, however, one feature is certain: David Cameron's **personal authority** has been enhanced considerably. Theories of prime ministerial power always include the fact that prime ministers are only as powerful, and only enjoy as much authority, as their political circumstances allow. By winning an election outright and by being able to cast off the constraints of coalition government, he is a considerably more powerful leader than he was before the election.

The new cabinet

The membership of the new cabinet as it was constituted by 9 May 2015 is shown in Table 9.1. It has a number of interesting features:

- It contains more women than recent Conservative or coalition cabinets. David Cameron has always claimed to be a 'moderniser' and this is seen as part of that characteristic.
- To a great extent it is ideologically united except over Europe. There are some members with a 'right-wing' reputation, such as Theresa May and Michael Gove but they are also Cameron loyalists.
- It may be that the issue of UK membership of the EU will divide this cabinet — it does contain some eurosceptics including May, Gove, Hammond and Fallon, but they may well come into line when the issue comes to a referendum. Most of the leading Conservative eurosceptics are not in the cabinet.
- The relationship between Cameron and Osborne is very close, bringing back memories of the Blair–Brown axis between 1997 and 2003. It may well be that this partnership will prove decisive in decision making. Few will dare to challenge the authority of a resurgent prime minister and a chancellor whose reputation has been growing fast.
- David Cameron has stated that he does not wish to remain prime minister for a third term. This means his successors will already be planning to take over. Several of the leading candidates are in the cabinet. These include Osborne, May and Gove. It may well be that they will become a problem for Cameron in 2 or 3 years' time.

Table 9.1 The cabinet members

Prime Minister	David Cameron, First Secretary of State
Chancellor of the Exchequer	George Osborne
Home Secretary	Theresa May
Foreign Secretary	Philip Hammond
Work and Pensions	Iain Duncan Smith
Defence	Michael Fallon
Chancellor of the Duchy of Lancaster	Oliver Letwin
Health	Jeremy Hunt
Chief Whip	Mark Harper
Leader of the House of Commons	Chris Grayling
Business	Sajid Javid
Justice	Michael Gove
Communities	Greg Clark
Education	Nicky Morgan
Energy and Climate Change	Amber Rudd
Culture, Media and Sport	John Whittingdale
Leader of the House of Lords	Baroness Stowell

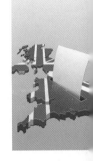

(continued)

Table 9.1 The cabinet members (continued)

Environment	Liz Truss
International Development	Justine Greening
Transport	Patrick McLoughlin
Northern Ireland	Theresa Villiers
Wales	Stephen Crabb
Scotland	David Mundell
Cabinet Office and Government Efficiency	Matthew Hancock

The following people are also entitled to attend cabinet meetings but are not cabinet ministers:

- Boris Johnson (no specific responsibility)
- Priti Patel (Employment)
- Anna Soubry (Small businesses)
- Robert Halfon (no specific role)
- Greg Hands (Chief Secretary to the Treasury)
- Baroness Anelay (Minister of State, Foreign Office)

When all cabinet ministers plus those entitled to attend but not full members meet, it is known as a 'political cabinet'.

This is the first cabinet David Cameron has been able to appoint without consulting another party. As such it is very much 'his' cabinet. He has kept on all the senior members of the former cabinet (apart from those retiring of their own accord) and, as such, they owe him an important debt of loyalty.

Europe and collective responsibility

It is a basic feature of the cabinet system that it is collectively responsible for all government policy and that no minister may publicly disagree with such policy. No sooner had the new cabinet taken its seats, however, than the issue of what to do about the forthcoming referendum on UK membership of the EU arose.

At first David Cameron appeared to be insisting that, when the referendum campaign starts, either in 2016 or 2017, all members of the cabinet will have to argue for a 'yes' vote (on the assumption that a favourable renegotiation of the UK's relationship with the EU will have been completed), whatever their personal views, or resign from government. Leading opponents of UK membership, such as John Redwood, immediately protested that this would bias the campaign decisively in favour of a 'stay in' vote and so the referendum would not be democratically legitimate, adding that such an assertion was too dictatorial. David Cameron responded quickly by changing his view, saying he would be considering this issue.

It remains to be seen whether collective cabinet responsibility will be suspended, perhaps for 30 days as some have suggested, during the referendum campaign. This is what occurred in 1975, the last time there was a public vote on membership of the European Community. Whatever happens, Europe remains the most problematic issue for the Conservative government — certainly until the people have had their say.

Conservatives for Britain

No sooner had the new government taken office than it found itself confronted by a new faction within the Conservative Party. Led by Steve Baker MP, this is known as **Conservatives for Britain**. Baker claimed that, before the end of June 2015, it had 110 MPs as members. This group is campaigning mainly for a 'fair' referendum campaign, for example insisting that there be a 1-month 'hiatus' on campaigning by the government. The faction also persuaded the prime minister to abandon plans to hold the referendum as early as 5 May 2016.

It is also supported by a former adviser to Michael Gove and an influential adviser to the Conservative Party, Dominic Cummings. Cummings is already gathering together supporters for a 'no' campaign which will include not only MPs, but also business leaders.

Until the referendum has taken place, therefore, it is likely that the new government will face as much obstruction from this faction as it will from the opposition parties.

Chapter 10

The Queen's Speech, May 2015

On 26 May the queen made her annual visit to Parliament to announce the government's plan for the forthcoming session. (This is known as the Queen's Speech, though it is written by the government.) It is customary for a new government to introduce most of its key measures early, before there is much possibility of obstruction and while it has a fresh mandate from the electorate. The announced programme says much about how the Conservatives intend to govern.

The new government's political programme for year one: key features

EU Referendum Bill

Legislation will pave the way for a referendum on British membership of the European Union, to be held by 2017. In the meantime the government will enter negotiations to reform the EU and change the nature of the UK's relationship with it.

Comment: This is perhaps the key element in the government's immediate political programme. It may well be that the referendum is brought forward to 2016, especially if David Cameron succeeds in gaining concessions from the EU. A referendum will also achieve two political objectives for the government. First, it will 'spike the UKIP guns'. Once the people have delivered their verdict on EU membership it will be difficult to see how UKIP will be able to retain public support. Second, it will outflank the large eurosceptic faction in the Conservative Party that threatens the stability of the government. If the UK leaves the EU, they will have little to complain about. If the vote is to stay in, they will be flying in the face of public opinion and, like UKIP, will lose support.

Full Employment and Welfare Benefits Bill

To some extent the legislation contains more of an aspiration than a set of specific proposals. It commits the government to creating 2 million more jobs and 3 million new apprenticeships. On the other hand, it reduces the government's benefits commitment. The overall cap on benefits to each family will be reduced from £26,000 per annum to £23,000. There will be a freeze on the levels of individual benefits for working people and for child benefit. Young people aged 18–21 will no longer have an automatic entitlement to housing benefit.

Comment: This bill is a double-edged sword. On the employment side it is a key part of what is coming to be known as 'blue collar conservatism' by extending employment and training opportunities. On the other hand, it restricts the level of welfare benefits which will affect poor families adversely. The reduction in benefits is designed both to help reduce the budget deficit and partly to make work more attractive, especially to the young.

Enterprise Bill

This is a commitment to cut regulations on small businesses and to simplify the system of business rates. It estimates that small business costs will be cut by £10 billion per year.

Comment: This is a rather vague commitment, but one that emphasises the Conservative claim to be the 'party of business'.

National Insurance Contributions and Finance Bill

This piece of legislation, unique in British political history, ensures that the government shall not be permitted to raise the rate of VAT, the rates of income tax and the level of National Insurance contributions up to 2020. It also makes a double commitment on tax for those on low pay. First, the rate at which people begin to pay income tax will be raised to an income of £12,500 per year. Second, anyone who works for 30 hours a week on minimum wage will not pay any income tax.

Comment: Never before has a British government passed legislation taking away its own powers to vary key tax rates. It is a response to charges that parties have, in the past, broken their election pledges on taxation. It is also another example of blue collar conservatism as the greatest benefit will be felt by those who are on lower incomes. However, critics point out that people who currently pay *no tax at all*, will gain nothing so it is divisive.

Childcare Bill

This will guarantee up to 30 hours of free childcare for 3–4-year-olds, for 38 weeks per year. Currently only 15 weekly hours are available.

Comment: A key pledge in the election campaign, this commitment is part of a policy of 'making work pay'. It will enable more parents of young children (realistically mostly women) to enter employment without having their income eroded by childcare costs. Again, this is an example of 'blue collar conservatism'.

Housing Bill

Tenants of housing association homes (1.3. million in number) will be entitled to buy their homes at a substantial discount. The housing associations will be compensated by local authorities who will find the money by selling off council properties. They will be committed to replacing all the homes sold under the scheme with new builds. The bill also contains a commitment to building 200,000 low-cost homes to be sold to under-40s at a 20% discount.

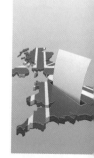

Comment: This is a highly controversial measure. Its critics argue that it will result in a reduction in the overall availability of low-cost housing as the homes sold simply cannot be replaced. The Conservatives see it as an extension of the plan to extend home ownership further, as started by

Margaret Thatcher's 1980s government which organised the sale of council homes to their tenants in what was known as the 'right to buy' scheme and which proved immensely popular.

Energy Bill

A new Oil and Gas Authority will be set up to regulate independently those two industries. More controversially, the power to exercise planning control over onshore wind farms will be transferred from central government to local authorities.

Comment: This is a very limited measure and may well result in a reduction in wind farm creation as so many local communities are reluctant to see such developments. It remains to be seen whether there is any significant effect on the relationship between energy firms and their customers.

Immigration Bill

This will create a new offence of 'illegal working', making it an offence to employ illegal immigrants and giving police the power to seize the wages of such workers. It will also require landlords to evict illegal immigrants. A new agency will be brought into existence to control illegal working. In particular, it will enforce a requirement that employers must not advertise jobs abroad before they are offered in the UK.

Comment: To some extent this proposal is a stopgap measure. David Cameron's real objective is to negotiate more extensive measures to control immigration from the EU. He has accepted that it will be difficult physically to stop most migrants entering the UK, so is concentrating on deterrent measures which will make the UK less attractive. It also fulfils a promise made to British workers that he will favour them when new jobs are being offered, largely as an answer to UKIP's appeal to low-paid workers and the unemployed.

Cities and Local Government Devolution Bill

This policy is very much part of the chancellor, George Osborne's agenda. It will transfer wide powers from central government to large cities, beginning with Greater Manchester. It will be a requirement that such partially self-governing cities will introduce elected mayors. Housing, transport, large-scale planning and policing will be devolved on a similar model to that adopted in London at the end of the last century.

Comment: Placed together with the proposals for devolution of more power to Scotland, Wales and Northern Ireland, city devolution represents part of a massive redistribution of power in the UK away from the centre. The Conservative party has traditionally been associated with the centralisation of power so this policy represents a major change of direction.

HS2 Bill

High Speed 2 (HS2) is a plan to build a £50-billion high-speed rail link between London and Birmingham and, in the future, to Manchester and beyond. The project will run between 2017 and 2026.

UK Government & Politics

Comment: This is a highly controversial measure on three levels. First, it has been criticised on the grounds of its cost. Second, many local communities along the proposed route have objected. Third, environmentalists see it as a major erosion of Britain's countryside. It is seen by the government as a key part of devolving power to big cities and to rebalance the economy, reversing the trend towards concentration on London and the southeast.

Scotland Bill, Wales Bill and Northern Ireland Bill

These three bills will pave the way for transferring considerable powers to these three countries. For Wales and Northern Ireland, these will be relatively modest, but Scotland is to be granted major powers over taxation and welfare. It may also be that David Cameron will negotiate even greater transfers of power than those recommended by the Smith Commission in 2014.

Comment: The Conservatives have recognised that further devolution is essential, especially in Scotland, where nationalist sentiment has grown. While critics have suggested that devolution will spell the end of the United Kingdom, David Cameron claims that such measures will head off demands for independence.

The Extremism Bill and Investigatory Powers Bill

This pair of bills is designed to combat the growing terrorist threat. The Extremism Bill will contain three main measures. First, it empowers OfCom (Office for Communications) to prevent broadcasting organisations airing programmes with 'extremist' messages. Second, extremist organisations will face banning orders if they engage in public provocation to extremism or racial or religious hatred. Third, it will give powers to the police to close down premises being used for extremist purposes.

The Investigatory Powers Bill will require mobile phone companies to keep records of calls, messages and images sent by their customers. These will then become available to security forces, as will internet records.

Comment: Both bills are highly controversial. Critics in the human rights community, liberals and members of the legal profession have said such laws are highly dangerous. Both they argue, will curtail freedom of speech and erode personal privacy. Too many of the new powers, they assert, are arbitrary and will require biased judgements about what constitutes 'extremism'. However, the government claims there is a great deal of public support for these measures and that they are essential to maintain the security of the country and keep law abiding citizens safe.

Trade Unions Bill

This legislation will require that, when a trade union ballots its members over strike action, there must be 50% approval for such action. In essential services, e.g. hospitals, fire and public transport, there will have to be at least a 40% turnout in such votes for the result to be valid.

Comment: This measure adds to curbs on trade unions introduced by Margaret Thatcher's Conservative governments in the 1980s. It will make it more difficult for large unionised groups of workers to use strikes to further their aims.

Other bills

In addition, bills are to be introduced to outlaw so-called 'legal highs', generally known as psychoactive substances, to deal with failing schools, to transfer control over bus services to local authorities and a number of other more technical proposals concerning the treatment of prisoners, the armed forces, adoption procedures and charities.

Overall assessment

This is an ambitious programme, designed to fulfil most of the Conservative Party's manifesto commitments as quickly as possible. This is normal practice for new governments. With a slender Commons majority, a potentially obstructive House of Lords and trouble brewing on the Scottish benches, the government needs to take the opportunity to pass its key measures while it remains strong. This programme aims to:

- deal with the issue of the UK's relationship with the European Union for the next generation to come
- decentralise power to Scotland, Wales, Northern Ireland and the big English cities
- give itself more powers to deal with the terrorist threat
- deal with the problem of immigration
- make work pay and so boost employment by reducing taxes on low incomes, reducing the benefits available for non-working people and families and by providing expanded free pre-school childcare
- encourage business to expand, notably smaller businesses
- expand home ownership

David Cameron claims that his party's programme represents a programme for 'ordinary working families' ('blue collar conservatism') and for national unity ('one nationism').

Critics of the programme will argue:

- There will be a significant increase in the powers of the state to invade our privacy and to curtail freedom of speech in the name of protection against terrorism.
- Far from being a 'one nation' programme, it may have the effect of breaking up the United Kingdom.
- The rights of workers will be further eroded, especially as there were no curbs proposed for zero-hours contracts.
- It will do little to reduce inequality as it does not propose increasing taxes on the wealthy.
- It will not solve the problem of a lack of house building, notably affordable housing.
- It does not include the details of the cuts in welfare benefits that will be needed if the budget deficit is to be reduced significantly (we may hear more in the July budget).

What about a British Bill of Rights?

In another sense, this programme is notable for what is missing as much as what is there. The government, at the last minute, dropped its proposal to repeal the Human Rights Act and replace it with a **British Bill of Rights**.

Supporters of this measure argued that the UK would regain control over rights, which are currently established and enforced by European judges. Parliament would again be fully sovereign over rights issues and the UK Supreme Court would again be the highest court of appeal. UK governments, they argue, are overly constrained by the European Convention on Human Rights.

Opponents saw it as a dangerous proposal. Human rights would be more vulnerable to actions by the UK government, using its control of the parliamentary majority possibly to erode rights, for example in the interests of national security or immigration control. In other words, rights were entrenched under the Human Rights Act but would cease to be so under a British Bill of Rights.

The government has realised that it faces strong opposition both from the House of Lords and from *within* the Conservative Party itself. Led by David Davis, a leading Conservative backbencher, the pro-rights faction threatens the government majority. The government also faced opposition outside Parliament, notably from Amnesty International and Liberty.

The Bill of Rights issue demonstrates the potential weakness of a government with such a small Commons majority and facing an active House of Lords, dominated by crossbenchers and opposition politicians. For now it has had to be postponed.

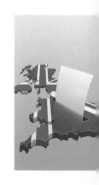

Chapter 11

A new politics?

Most commentators accept that politics in the UK has changed radically since 2010. The old model of two parties battling each other for a larger share of the 'centre ground', while preserving their own solid, core support, with a small third party trying to gain some traction and occasionally succeeding, seems to have gone. In particular, the three main parties can no longer rely on that traditional old core support that gave them such an advantage over smaller aspiring parties. Voters are more volatile, willing to support new parties and looking for which party will advantage them to the greatest degree.

In addition, politics in the UK has never been more regional. The election results demonstrate that Scotland is now firmly in nationalist hands, the North is still Labour dominated while the South, including the East but excluding London, is almost totally Conservative. Genuine two or more party politics only really exists in London, the Midlands and Wales. Given these developments, there are three models of politics in the UK that may emerge in the near future.

Possible future models of politics in the UK

Model 1: a fragmented electorate and party system

There were very distinctive voting patterns in most areas:

- Scotland (SNP dominated)
- London and the big Midland and Northern cities (Labour dominated)
- the North East (also Labour dominated)
- rural and suburban areas in all regions of England and Wales (Conservative dominated)
- the South in general (almost exclusively Conservative)
- the East including Essex, Kent, Suffolk and Norfolk (strong UKIP showing despite winning only one seat)

There were also pockets of strong support for the Green Party (Brighton, Norwich, parts of London).

If this pattern continues it will remain difficult for one of the big parties to gain a decisive majority — possibly no majority at all, as occurred in 2010. Furthermore, traditional class-based voting broke down even more than in the recent past. For example, UKIP seems to have taken as much support away from Labour as it did from the Conservatives. The traditional working class is shrinking; ethnic minorities, who in the past supported Labour in large numbers, are now more willing to vote Conservative. The under-30s still tend to vote centre-left, but many also vote Green. The male 30–49 age group was most solidly Conservative (other than pensioners), but women still tend to favour Labour.

This new landscape might result in a permanent multi-party system, especially, of course, if proportional representation were introduced to entrench the party system. The UK would then have to get used to the idea of power-sharing governments and consensus politics. This model would have to result in radical changes in the way government and Parliament operate and interact with each other.

Model 2: regional politics

Two forces are at work here. The first is the noticeable increase in regional variations in voting patterns and therefore support for different parties. There has always been a 'North–South' divide in party support in the UK, but the pattern is now more complex, notably the way in which Scotland, London, the big cities and Wales resisted the drift towards greater Conservative support.

The second change concerns the decentralisation of power, both national devolution and the transfer of responsibilities to big city regions such as Manchester and Birmingham. This decentralisation will facilitate regional variations in party support. It may well be in the future that Scotland and Wales plus the city regions will be dominated and therefore governed by parties of the centre-left, i.e. nationalists or Labour, while the rest of the country will be Conservative dominated. This is the kind of politics that exists in Germany, a federal system, where typically the Northern *Länder* (provinces) return Social Democrat governments, while the South is more conservative. Italy, not a federal system, has similar regional variations, making it difficult to govern from the centre. Spain, recognising the problem of its geographical variations in culture and economic structure, has granted considerable devolution to its several regions.

A further refinement of this model might occur if big-city devolution does take place. It is likely that all big-city mayors and governments would be controlled by Labour (assuming general election results are generally replicated in mayoral elections). Even London may fall into Labour hands after 2016 when Boris Johnson stands down. This presents a picture of a Conservative national government faced by powerful Labour strongholds in partly self-governing cities. In other words, the checks and balances on central government may, in future, not come from *within* Westminster, but from the cities and the national regions.

Model 3: the US model

An outlying possibility is that the British electorate will soon tire of such fragmentation and want a return to single-party government. This would be signalled by a noticeable abandonment of support for smaller parties and a return to two-party dominance. The two parties would be one of the centre-left, progressive and liberal variety (Democrats in the USA); while the other would be conservative (like the US Republicans). There would then be no room for small parties and elections would be won and lost on shifts in the preferences of a small group of swing voters. One of the two main parties would always govern, and govern alone.

As in the USA, where FPTP is used for congressional elections, the electoral system underpins two-party dominance. The failure of the Greens and UKIP to make a breakthrough and the collapse of Liberal Democrat support may well point to this development in the future. Scotland is, of course, a special case, which may become less significant after more devolution or even disappear altogether with full independence.

Changes in UK society

Whatever happens in the next generation British politics is unlikely ever to be the same again. The question is: how much change will there be? Two other societal changes, though, should be observed if we are to find clues as to how politics will change in the future. The first is the degree to which the problem of inequality, in terms of living standards and opportunities, continues to grow. If inequality does become more pronounced, there may well be a return to ideological politics as social conflict grows. The second is the impact of the growing ethnic diversity of the UK. The prospect of 'ethnic politics' opens the door to many new possibilities.

The future of party politics in the UK

Finally some questions need to be asked about the future of party politics in the UK. Among them are these:

- Which direction will Labour take? Will it move to the centre and seek to compete with the Conservatives on their own strong ground or will it shift even further to the left in order to stem the leakage of support in Scotland and the North of England? If it chooses wrongly it may be consigned to opposition for a generation.
- Will UKIP survive after the referendum on UK membership of the EU? Whether the voters say yes or no to membership, the main issue on which it fights will be removed. It is difficult to imagine the party continuing to campaign for a UK exit if the people vote to stay in. If the UK leaves it has also lost its main policy. Furthermore, if the UK stays in the EU it will seem impossible to make substantial changes to the immigration rules.
- What now for the Liberal Democrats? They face an uphill battle to restore their position. If the two largest parties manage to retain their support in their key areas, it is difficult to see how they will be able to attract voters again. On the other hand, with strong new leadership, they may be able to find a distinctive political position.
- What next for the SNP? Their prospects look very bright. There will be elections to the Scottish Parliament next year and the party is set to dominate again. If the SNP retains its dominant position we may see a new campaign for independence. Its only real rival in Scotland is Labour. If a popular devolution settlement is reached with the new UK government Labour may have an opportunity to recover.

One thing seems certain. Party politics has changed for the foreseeable future.

UK Government & Politics

Summary

Students of politics should find much of interest in the result and outcome of the 2015 general election. The following is a summary of how our knowledge of various topics can be amended and updated by this election, including what issues to look out for in the future.

Democracy in the UK

- Once again a peaceful, well-ordered election demonstrates the stability of democracy in the UK.
- The losers in the election accepted the authority of the winners to govern, although this can now be questioned in Scotland. There was a peaceful transition of power from one government to the next, a vital principle of government.
- Again, however, we saw the problems thrown up by the first-past-the-post electoral system (see below under 'The electoral system').
- The most serious challenge to UK democracy came with the Scottish situation. The governing party won only 1 seat out of 59 in Scotland. The question therefore arises: is the UK government legitimate in Scotland? It is for this reason that the government will be forced to negotiate a new settlement with the SNP. To a lesser extent the same situation arises in Wales, though nationalism there is much weaker than in Scotland.

Representation

- The new House of Commons is somewhat more socially representative than the old one. There was an increased intake of women compared to 2010 — up from 148 to 187 — though this is relatively slow progress. Of the 56 SNP MPs, 20 are women. More progress has been made on ethnicity, with a rise of MPs from ethnic minorities up from 27 to 41. This number is approaching the national average for ethnicity.
- David Cameron's new cabinet is also more socially balanced, though 57% of the membership was still educated at private schools. Ten women are now in cabinet or entitled to attend some meetings. This is a major advance towards gender balance. Two members of the full cabinet are from an ethnic minority — Sajid Javid and Priti Patel.
- The House of Commons is as unrepresentative of party support as it ever was. Labour and the Conservatives are heavily over-represented, as is the SNP. On the other hand, UKIP is under-represented as badly as any party has ever been in history, including the Liberal Democrats. The Green Party also should have several more members, given its public support.

Political participation

- Despite the closeness of the prospective outcome, turnout remained low in historical terms, at just over 66%, slightly up since 2010. The decline in voting turnout does seem to have been arrested, but there is no improvement.
- Turnout in Scotland was higher than in the rest of the UK, at 71%. This may well have been because many people were more engaged in politics as a result of the 2014 Scottish independence referendum, when nearly 90% of the electorate there voted.

The electoral system

- The new majority government secured just under 37% of the popular vote. The Conservative Party increased its vote by only 0.8% but this was translated into 25 additional seats, enough to secure its majority. This demonstrates how FPTP exaggerates support for some parties.
- Again, as in most elections, the legitimacy of the government can be challenged on the basis that it was elected on only 36% of the popular vote.
- The party that benefited most from FPTP, however, was the SNP which converted 50% of the popular vote into over 94% of the seats in Scotland. Interestingly, though the SNP gained hugely by FPTP, the party's policy supports the introduction of proportional representation for the whole of the UK.
- The party that lost out most seriously from FPTP was UKIP. It gained 12.6% of the popular vote (mostly in England), but won only one seat. Note that the Liberal Democrats were significantly less discriminated against by the system than UKIP.
- Nevertheless, the outcome may mute the demands for the introduction of proportional representation. This is partly because the Conservative Party is opposed to such a change, and partly because FPTP has restored its reputation for producing single-party government with an overall majority so there is less impetus for change. Had FPTP produced two indecisive results in a row, demands for a change would have been greater. But that did not happen.

Voting behaviour

It will take some time before research is conducted into trends in voting behaviour. However, the early data from the election suggest the following trends:

- The tendency of traditional working-class voters to support Labour may be weakening. A *Survation* survey carried out in the days after the election discovered that UKIP had attracted many former Labour voters, especially in the North of England.
- The tendency for voters to become more Conservative in their outlook as they grow older remains a key factor in voting behaviour.
- Early indications are that the old adage that, *it's the economy that counts*, still holds true. Voters who did not have a strong party allegiance do appear to have been influenced by the Conservative campaign which stressed its own sound economic record compared to Labour's past incompetence.
- Ethnicity is now less of a clue to an individual's voting intentions.

The party system

- It was already established before the election that the UK now has a multi-party system. The election did not change this, though some may argue that the two-party system has re-established itself outside Scotland, especially with the collapse in support for the Liberal Democrats.
- Some have argued that the UK does indeed have a multi-party system, but this is different in the various parts of the UK, i.e. England has a four-party system, (Con/Lab/UKIP/Lib Dem, with the Greens still struggling to make an impact), Scotland has a four-party system (SNP/Lab/Con/Lib Dem), Wales has a similar four-party system, but including Plaid Cymru. This analysis is based on the possibility that the Liberal Democrats do recover and again become a force in British politics.
- One-party dominance in Scotland certainly exists, though this may well be a temporary phenomenon.

Party policies

- The Conservative party is now established as a modern, moderate, just-right-of-centre party, as envisaged by David Cameron. Its policies were described by Cameron, shortly after his re-election, as a 'one nation' party.
- The term **'blue collar Toryism'** is now being given to the leading members of the Conservative Party. This is a policy position designed to appeal largely to the aspirational working classes as well as the existing middle classes, including those who run small businesses. Its main policies include cutting direct taxes on middle incomes, providing more affordable housing, cutting welfare to increase incentives to work, maintaining free, unregulated labour markets and providing more apprenticeships to encourage skills development.
- David Cameron has also referred to governing for 'one nation'. This appears to be partly a claim to represent all classes in society and also to resist those forces which now threaten the unity of the United Kingdom.
- Nevertheless, there is a significant right-wing faction in the Conservative Party, numbering about 50 MPs. This group will cause problems for the government as they now effectively hold the balance of power. The Conservative majority of only 12 is not enough to keep them in check. This group will want to see an exit from the EU, strict immigration controls, deep tax cuts and large reductions in the scope of the welfare state.
- The failure of UKIP to convert its support into more than one seat gives Cameron the opportunity to resist right-wing demands to head off that challenge.
- Labour must now reconsider its position. Most commentators suggest its loss was because its policies were too 'left wing'. This suggests, therefore, that the party needs to move back to a centrist, 'New Labour' or 'Blairite' position, appealing to the aspirational middle classes as well as the working classes. However, Labour lost Scotland to a radical party of the left, the SNP. If the party does move to centrist policies, it may lose Scotland for good. Some union chiefs are also warning against Labour moving to the centre and abandoning its traditional working-class roots.

- The Liberal Democrats will probably continue to present themselves as a radical alternative to the two-party system, stressing the protection of rights, democratisation and social justice. They will feel freer to do this as they are no longer in coalition.

The constitution, devolution and the EU

- The proposal for a British Bill of Rights, if it is implemented (there may be fierce opposition to this) will have the effect of restoring parliamentary sovereignty which had been eroded by the European Convention on Human Rights as this has tended to be superior to parliamentary legislation.
- Clearly, if Britain were to leave the EU following the referendum in 2016 or 2017, there would be profound constitutional effects, not least the further restoration of parliamentary sovereignty.
- The fact that the SNP does not hold the balance of power in the House of Commons somewhat weakens its influence. This means its demands for constitutional reform have less leverage.
- However, the huge SNP win in Scotland means that the question of a new relationship between Scotland (and therefore Wales and Northern Ireland too) and the UK has been opened. This means that the Conservative government will have to consider how to achieve this. Certainly it seems likely that there will be a great extension of devolution. This is likely to include autonomy over taxation and public expenditure.
- Some are even proposing that the new political landscape suggests the need for a federal system, where sovereignty will be transferred to Scotland, Wales and Northern Ireland, and that England will have its own separate political institutions.
- The West Lothian question will now be more acute, with 56 SNP members in the Commons. Will they be allowed to vote on issues that *only* affect England (EVEL — English Votes for English Laws)? This will also be the subject of future negotiations.

The prime minister and the executive

- Clearly the prime minister now has more authority than when he led a coalition. His powers of patronage are fully restored and he commands a Commons majority.
- However, he only has a majority of 12, the smallest government majority since 1974. This means that even a minor revolt in his party will prevent him seeing proposals through Parliament.
- David Cameron has enhanced authority, having pulled off such an unexpected but impressive win. This should give him more control over his cabinet. However, his insistence that he will not seek a third term may well weaken him as time goes by.

UK Government & Politics

Parliament

- The key question for the new Parliament is going to be the West Lothian question and EVEL (see above).
- The issue of Lords reform may well take a back seat for some time. The Conservative Party does have Lords reform as part of its official policy (it was in its manifesto in 2015) but there are many other issues to be resolved in the Parliament so the political will for reform may be lacking.
- There is a problem for the government as it faces a large majority *against* it in the Lords and the prime minister will not be able to fill up the Lords with enough Conservative peers to correct this, so expects some obstruction in the Lords. The repeal of the Human Rights Act and its replacement by a British Bill of Rights may well have a rough ride in the Lords.
- The narrowness of the government majority means that Parliament may not continue to be as influential as it was between 2010 and 2015. It must be remembered that the new government has a much smaller majority in the Commons than the coalition enjoyed.
- It will only take a few by-election losses or defections to other parties for the government to lose its majority. This will transform the role and influence of Parliament.
- The House of Commons remains socially unrepresentative, but some limited progress has been made towards redressing the gender and ethnic balance of the House.

Civil liberties and the judiciary

- A major proposal in the Conservative party manifesto was a commitment to repeal the Human Rights Act and replace the European Convention on Human Rights (ECHR) with a British Bill of Rights. This would have represented a major transfer of sovereignty away from the European Court of Human Rights back to the UK Parliament and the UK Supreme Court. However, this was immediately postponed in the face of fierce opposition from within the Conservative Party, the new cabinet and the House of Lords. It may well prove to be the first piece of evidence of how potentially weak the new government is.
- The anti-terror laws being introduced in the next year will give the security forces and the police wide powers to intercept mobile phone and internet messages in the interests of gathering intelligence on potential and actual terrorists. It will also give the police powers to close down meetings and premises used to propagate 'extreme views'. Students should follow the course of this legislation as it may well be fought over in both houses of Parliament.

Examination questions

Listed below are some typical examination questions, in both short and long format, where the outcome of the election can provide useful fresh examples and new insights.

Short questions

1 Explain the impact of the first-past-the-post system.
2 Explain the concept of the electoral mandate.
3 Explain three functions of general elections.
4 Outline methods that have been proposed to increase turnout at elections.
5 In what senses does the UK have a two-party system?
6 Outline three policies on which the Labour and Conservative parties disagreed in the 2015 election campaign.
7 Outline three policies on which there was political consensus in 2015.
8 Explain, with examples, the meaning of devolution.
9 Briefly outline the meaning of the West Lothian question.
10 Explain three sources of prime ministerial authority.
11 What factors does a prime minister consider when appointing cabinet members?
12 Outline three ways in which the House of Commons is a representative body.

Long questions

1 To what extent do general elections in the UK enhance democracy?
2 How and to what extent was the 2011 referendum on electoral reform unsatisfactory, while the 2014 referendum on Scottish independence was satisfactory?
3 To what extent do general election results since 2000 indicate the need for electoral reform?
4 To what extent is the UK now a multi-party system?
5 Has the Conservative Party now returned to its 'one nation' roots?
6 To what extent is Labour still a left-wing party?
7 How and why did Labour and the Liberal Democrats 'lose' the 2015 general election?
8 What constitutional problems have arisen from the recent rise of Scottish nationalism?
9 To what extent are civil liberties under threat from recent and proposed legislation?
10 How representative is the UK Parliament today?
11 'UK prime ministers have become weaker since 2005.' Do you agree?
12 How successful was coalition government between 2010 and 2015?

      UK Government & Politics